A Cry for Dignity

Religion and Violence

Series Editors
Lisa Isherwood, University of Winchester, and Rosemary Radford Ruether,
Graduate Theological Union, Berkeley, California

This interdisciplinary and multicultural series brings to light the ever increasing problem of religion and violence. The series will highlight how religions have a significant part to play in the creation of cultures that allow and even encourage the creation of violent conflict, domestic abuse and policies and state control that perpetuate violence to citizens.

The series will highlight the problems that are experienced by women during violent conflict and under restrictive civil policies. But not wishing to simply dwell on the problems the authors in this series will also re-examine the traditions and look for alternative and more empowering readings of doctrine and tradition. One aim of the series is to be a powerful voice against creeping fundamentalisms and their corrosive influence on the lives of women and children.

Published:

Forthcoming:

A Cry for Dignity

*Religion, Violence and the Struggle of
Dalit Women in India*

Mary C. Grey

LONDON   OAKVILLE

Published by Equinox Publishing Ltd.

UK: 1 Chelsea Manor Studios, Flood Street, London, SW3 5SR
USA: DBBC, 28 Main Street, Oakville, CT 06779

www.equinoxpub.com

First published 2010

British Library Cataloguing-in-Publication Data
A catalogue record for this book is available from the British Library.

ISBN-13   978 184553 605 3   (hardback)
          978 184553 606 0   (paperback)

Library of Congress Cataloging-in-Publication Data

Grey, Mary C
A cry for dignity: religion, violence, and the struggle of Dalit
women in India/Mary Grey.
     p. cm. — (Religion and violence)
  Includes bibliographical references and index.
    ISBN 978-1-84553-605-3 (hb) — ISBN 978-1-84553-606-0 (pb) 1.
Dalits — India — Social conditions. 2. Dalits — Religious life — India. 3.
Women — India — Social conditions. 4. Women — Religious life — India. I.
Title. DS422.C3G74 2010
305.48'994 — dc22
                              2010000019

Typeset by S.J.I. Services, New Delhi
Printed and bound in Great Britain by Lightning Source UK Ltd, Milton Keynes

CONTENTS

Foreword and Acknowledgments

I owe debts to many people whom I want to acknowledge and thank as fellow campaigners in this particular struggle. Not the least is Professor James Massey of the Centre for Dalit/Subaltern Studies and his team in New Delhi – frequently mentioned in this book. Second, I would like to thank Meena Varma, Director of the Dalit Solidarity Network in London, the whole team, and its founder Revd David Haslam. I am also grateful to Professors Rosemary Ruether and Lisa Isherwood, series editors, for giving me this opportunity to develop work in this area.

But there is one person to whom I want to dedicate this work: this is the late L.C. Tyagi, an inspiring Gandhian activist whom Nicholas and I had the privilege to know and work with for 10 years. He, with his wife, Mrs Shashi Tyagi, also an outstanding leader, especially of women, founded *Gravis,*[1] an NGO devoted to the poorest people in the Thar Desert of Rajasthan. Sadly, Tyagiji, as he was respectfully known, died three years ago, exhausted from a lifetime of overwork and commitment to the wellbeing of his people, but the work carries on through his son Dr Prakash Tyagi, his wife, Dr Vasundhera and their dedicated team. It was Tyagiji's vision and wisdom that encouraged me to look again at what Gandhi's ideas could offer for the struggle of Dalit women today. This book is a small offering to his memory.

In this book The poem 'Mother' by Waman Nimbalkar originally published in *Poisoned Bread* by Arjun Dangle is reproduced with prior permission from Orient Blackswan Private Limited, Hyderabad, Andhra Pradesh, India.

---

1. Gramin Vikas Vigyan Samiti, Village Self-help Organization.

A Cry for Dignity

Poetry extracts from *The Silken Swing: The Cultural Universe of Dalit Women* edited by Fernando Franco, Jyotsna Macwan and Suguna Ramanathan are reproduced by permission of the publisher Stree, Kolkata, India. © Behavioural Science Centre, St. Xavier's College, Ahmedabad, 2000.

My thanks also to Oxford University Press for granting permission to reprint an extract from Janabai's poem: "Caste off all Shame"; and to Aruna Gnanadason for granting permission to reprint her poem, "They Heal their Bodies ... They Heal the Earth".

INTRODUCTION

Five years ago I wrote a small book, *The Unheard Scream: The Struggle of Dalit Women in India.*[1] Many strands had come together in its writing and the seriousness of the social situation and its very refusal to disappear have prompted this second attempt, this time from the angle of religion and violence. (It had also been problematic that the book's circulation hardly spread outside India). *Dalit* is the name that the former Untouchables of India and other Asian countries have chosen for themselves. It means 'broken' or 'crushed' – like lentils, and lentil *dal* is a well-known popular dish. Although I am neither Indian nor Dalit, the nature of this outrageous form of oppression and violence cries out for international solidarity and action – as has become evident in International Conferences on Human Rights, the World Social Forum, and increasingly, the courageous protests of thousands of Dalits, both women and men. It has also become an outrage that after the Tsunami Relief of 2006 that Dalits were by–passed and ignored in the distribution of relief and other forms of aid.

Second, my own involvement – for 23 years – as Founder Trustee of the Non Governmental Organisation,[2] *Wells for India,* has brought the issue very much to the fore as an obstacle to development, change and gender justice. This commitment has meant visiting every year three very diverse drought-affected areas of rural Rajasthan (north-west India) meeting with the village people and the Field Workers of our partners, participating in drought relief and holistic development projects, as well as more long-term social

1. Published by the Centre for Dalit Studies, New Delhi, by Professor James Massey and his team.
2. Non Governmental Organisations are legally constituted and operate independently of the government.

change issues.[3] My own focus has been especially with gender justice and the difficulties that the women of Rajasthan face in changing the quality of their lives for the better, their situation being recognized by their own State Government as an 'international issue.' Within this patriarchal and caste-dominated context the position of Dalit women is even more serious and intractable. It has become ever clearer that gender justice and caste oppression are closely intertwined, as I hope to show.

Very slowly our team in *Wells for India* has begun to understand the complexity of the struggle the village people, especially the women, are engaged in; that it was not just drought and poverty they faced, harsh though these realities definitely are: when caste issues and the burden of a deeply rooted patriarchy are factored into the situation, the odds stacked against the people we are involved with – tribals (such as Bhils, Meena, Garasia) scheduled castes like the Meghwals, as well as other low caste and former Untouchables themselves – begin to appear insuperable. Especially for the women of rural villages, often isolated from the benefits of education and progress. The State Government of Rajasthan itself, in its report of 1999, in declaring that the plight of its women is an international issue (as mentioned above) clarified many of the areas of suffering, such as maternal and infant mortality, female infanticide and sexual violence. It announced a range of measures in response, but *caste issues were not factored in.*

In the Thar Desert, north of Jodhpur (one of the areas most severely hit by the relentless five year drought, only relieved by the monsoon of summer 2003) our Gandhian partners from an organization called Gramin Vikas Vigyan Samiti (*Gravis*) struggle daily with the realities of caste in implementing their projects. In fact, when they began work in this area of Rajasthan in 1986, all their offices were burnt down, so great was the fury of the high-caste people (known as Rajputs in this area) that they had made low-caste and tribal people the focus of their work.[4] One focus of

3. *Wells for India* works with Gramin Vikas Vigyan Samiti (*Gravis*) whose office is in Jodhpur, and with ten project implementing partners in the Aravali Hills south of Udaipur. New projects are starting elsewhere. We have a small office in Udaipur (Rajasthan).
4. This story is told by William Dalrymple in *The Age of Kali* (New York: HarperCollins, 1998).

this study will be to explore the different attitudes to caste and in particular to women of the two great reformers, Gandhi, and the less well-known but far more significant for Dalits, Dr 'Babasaheb' Ambedkar, himself a Dalit and a founder of the Indian Constitution, a much ignored achievement.

The third motivating strand is that, as a Roman Catholic woman theologian, my work for the last 25 years has been in the area of social justice, especially in diverse Liberation and Feminist Theologies. Increasingly, my focus has become justice for women,[5] as well as an ecofeminist orientation, exploring how justice for women and the earth are intrinsically interlinked. Land ownership issues are particularly relevant here, and a specific source of suffering for Dalit people. My own study of Dalit *theology*, the lives of Dalit Christians and their experiences of Christian Church has been particularly resourced by the extensive work of the Dalit theologian, Prof. James Massey and his colleagues Father Lourdeswamy, Father Monodeep Daniel, Sister Shalini Malakal and Mr Pramod at the new Centre for Dalit/Subaltern Studies in Delhi. With this team we – a group of *Wells for India* supporters – also visited some Dalit colonies in the city slums. This visit made a deep impression on all of us, especially as we had visited a colony of people formerly from Rajasthan and could see for ourselves what happens to landless people when they are forced to migrate to the city. These people were also facing a further upheaval – forced to make way for the expanding international airport in Delhi. The Centre possessed many books which the team had written on Dalit history, theology and the Dalit struggle – but nothing on women, although again and again we had been told that women were 'the Dalits of the Dalits', the 'thrice Dalits', and represented the area of greatest suffering of the Dalit people as a whole. My initial book was a first attempt to plug this gap, in the hope that Dalit women will themselves write their life stories and struggles. This book builds on the first attempt, influenced also by other factors, especially by the work of the Centre for Dalit Rights (CDR) in Rajasthan, based in Jaipur, and its dedicated team.

The most important of the changing factors in the situation is that in the last 10 years India – along with China – has increasingly

5. See, M. Grey, *Redeeming the Dream: Christianity, Feminism and Redemption* (Gujarat: Gujarat Sahitya Prakash, 2000).

become an influential player on the world scene. As I write, the world has entered a global recession and it is unclear how long this will last and with what effects. Money has been poured into huge development projects. A former Prime Minister of India, Sri Vaj Payee, invented the term 'Shining India' to describe his attempts to improve India's international profile by a network of motorways, opening up of airports and encouraging international corporations to operate in India. One consequence of this has been the opportunities for employment within companies who have 'outsourced' to India, and the caste situation has again raised its head. Thus through the efforts of the Dalit Solidarity Network UK[6] (DSN) – in conjunction with the International Dalit Solidarity Network (IDSN) – the Ambedkar Principles have been produced,[7] to regulate and monitor employment of Dalits in these companies. This needs to be placed within the wider consequences of globalization for Dalits – a recurring theme of this book.

The theme of this Equinox book series, 'Religion and Violence', also provides a key frame. It is not only that justice for the Dalit people and Dalit women specifically has not received sufficient attention within Liberation Theology; but it has not been fully acknowledged that it is the foundation and structures of religion that are responsible for the enduring injustices of the caste system. To challenge its foundations is to challenge the roots of Hinduism, so it is claimed, and is one of the *reasons why Dalit oppression remains the dark underside of 'Shining India'*. In these days of inter-faith dialogue, it has seemed an easier solution to try to eradicate some of the worst features of caste oppression without challenging these roots. To tackle this will take us out of the frame of Christian theology, exploring the extent to which Dalit women receive solace or oppression from Hindu religion (and other forms of spirituality) and what the experience of Dalits became when many of them, following Dr Ambedkar in 1956, converted to Buddhism.

In the long run, Dalit women will liberate themselves, but if through our Human Rights organizations nationally and internationally we can help the process by raising awareness, both politically and in faith circles, and by our global solidarity, then that is something that must be tackled from many contexts and

6. I am a patron of this organization.
7. See Appendix A.

not only in India. Caste oppression is alive and well in other countries too.

So the question becomes: is it possible from this distance, from this comfortable Western situation, then, to step into the *chappals* (sandals) of a Dalit woman, aware too, that *chappals* can be used as a term of derision against Dalit women, who are forced to perform humiliating tasks with inadequate or no shoes. And if through empathy and solidarity it becomes possible to some degree, can we begin to see how all the issues of untouchability, purity and pollution, endogamy and access to the essentials of life adversely affect specifically the lives of Dalit women in a way different from men? And, third, as a result of these explorations what are the specific actions of solidarity needed for the liberation of Dalit women?

Responses will necessarily be diverse and complex. After trying to understand the realities of caste oppression, and then specifically as it affects the lives of Dalit women in the specific areas of injustice such as domestic violence and sexual harassment, I will then open up an exploration as to the ways religion acts as oppressor or tool for liberation. A specifically *Christian* theological response addresses the ways the Church has failed to speak to the situation of Dalit women – and failed the Dalit community as a whole. But has Buddhism succeeded any better? This is a question that needs investigating. And what should be the role and contribution of Feminist Theology in terms of solidarity and protest?

In so doing I realize this will be one response among many, one voice that aims *not to speak for Dalit women* but to try to make their voices and their struggles known in different parts of the world. Part of the purpose of this book is that justice, dignity and flourishing for Dalit women will be taken seriously by the global Women's Movement. Second, it will reveal the part religion is playing in blocking the end to sexual violence against women. But it is also a cry of protest that women should have to endure such humiliation in the daily round of ordinary life: the hope is that in the protest are the seeds of resistance and change and an end to what could be the cruellest and most ancient form of oppression in the world, again, especially for women.

Chapter 1

Caste in a Culture of Globalization

> To be human is to recognise that Dalit woman is *someone*, someone
> who matters, is significant, who cannot be forgotten or be absent,
> or invisible in our society. She is the subject of history and the
> future of humanity lies in her hands and in her heart.[1]

The above quotation sets out a challenge: to begin to answer it, this
chapter aims to open up basic issues and contexts of life for Dalit
people in general and women in particular, issues to be explored
later, in greater depth.

What is Caste?

> Caste is a form of slavery that has throughout history
> systematically organised many races of people in the world,
> having been used as a system to discriminate between different
> tribes and races of people living in the same geographical area.
> Most of the ancient civilisations, including Africa, Greece, Rome
> and China, used some form of caste system to determine who is
> superior and who is inferior. What distinguishes caste in India
> from that in most countries is that *Indian caste divisions are
> sanctioned by religion* and it's a graded inequality (*my italics*).[2]

But the second distinguishing feature of caste in India is that whereas
in other civilizations and the history of development of different
nations, due to the processes of industrialization, development,
democratization and educational reform, caste has almost
disappeared, (although class structures still linger on), in India and
some other Asian countries this has not happened. This is despite
the fact that the Indian government made caste illegal in 1950. Nor

---

1. Fr Leo Sequeira, 'Human Responses to Dalit Women Today', in P.G.
Jogdand (ed.), *Dalit Women in India: Issues and Perspectives* (New Delhi: Gyan
Publishing House, 1995), pp. 122–34, quotation p. 130.
    2. Valerie Mason-John, *Broken Voices: Untouchable Women Speak Out* (New
Delhi: India Research Press, 2008), p. 1.

is it only in India that caste oppression flourishes. Dalit theologian James Massey, in his many publications, has estimated that there are 300m Dalits worldwide, not only in India, but in Pakistan, Bangladesh and Nepal. Types of caste systems also exist in countries like Africa. This figure of 300m Dalits – or 'Dalit *bahujans'* (the wider family) as they are known – include tribal peoples, scheduled castes and Other Backward castes, or OBCs. Tribal people are the indigenous peoples of India, largely forced into the hills at the Aryan invasion.[3] But more recently, since India's Independence (1947), deforestation and the logging of trees on a massive scale removed the livelihood of many of these people, who now must struggle to earn a living in the valleys and villages, or even more difficult, in the towns. Some estimates of the number of Dalits include the *sudras*[4] too – the lowest rung of the caste system – and 75 percent of this group – some figures say 80 percent – are below the poverty line (BPL).

In addition, caste oppression follows Dalits when they leave India in the hope of escaping caste. A recent piece of research commissioned by the Dalit Solidarity Network in Britain (henceforth DSN) in July 2006 began to disclose the extent of this:

> Approximately 50,000 Dalits live in the UK. Exact figures are unknown due to issues around identification as a "Dalit", and the changing of names. Caste is not currently recognised as a form of discrimination in UK legislation. However the government is currently reviewing all forms of discrimination in the UK in preparation for the drafting of the Single Equality Act.[5]

> Despite the limitations and scope of this research certain sectors clearly emerge as key areas of concern. *These include discrimination in employment, education and religious institutions, particularly in relation to access to temples*[6] (My italics).

3. This will be discussed later.
4. To be explained below and in more detail in Chapters 2 and 3. For DSN, see www.dsnuk.org
5. http://www.theequalitiesreview.org.uk/
6. This research has been carried out as part of DSN's ongoing work in raising the issue of caste discrimination with the Commission for Racial Equality, the Foreign and Commonwealth Office and the Home Office in the UK. These institutions have indicated that they are currently looking into the presence and impact of such discrimination and whether it should be incorporated into existing equality laws in the UK.

This report clearly illustrates that caste discrimination exists in the UK. DSN believes that it is as unacceptable as any other form of discrimination and that policy makers, community groups and the judiciary must work together to ensure its eradication.

One clear example from the Report will serve to illustrate this. The Mayor of Coventry,[7] Ram Lakha, a Labour Councillor who is a Dalit, faced intense discrimination from upper-caste Indians when he stood for election in a largely Indian ward:

During campaigning I was often told that I would not get people's vote as I was a chamar[8] (regarded as a derogatory name for Dalits and referring to one of the castes lower in the hierarchy). So I filed my nomination in a non-Asian constituency and was able to win. The Indian Community in Coventry always felicitates every new Mayor; however, till today they have not done this for me.

This report urges the Home Office, the Department of Education and the Secretary of State for Work and Pensions in particular, to prioritize this issue and to work together with organizations like DSN to raise awareness and develop recommendations to address this issue.

The name *Dalit* (as the introduction explained) means 'broken' or crushed. Like the *dal* – a universally popular dish made from lentils – where the lentils must be crushed to produce the sauce, the Dalits see themselves as broken people, deliberately crushed by the caste system. They reject as paternalistic and patronizing the name 'Harijan' (children of God) given to them by Mahatma Gandhi. This name even has connotations of temple prostitution. 'Dalit' is the Dalit self-chosen name and inspires their campaign for social change and liberation.

The origins of caste are disputed, lost in the mists of history and will be discussed more fully later. But as the focus of this book is the intractability of the issue because of its religious underpinning, the connection needs to be made clear from the beginning. It is not only the area of Untouchability that is rooted in religion, but the entire social order associated with Hinduism. As James Massey writes:

7. Mr Ram Lakha was Mayor at the time when the research was conducted.
8. The chamars are traditionally a street-sweeping caste.

The story of the present social order of India had its historical roots in one of the earliest war conflicts, which took place between the first settlers of ancient India and the late comers. The second group addressed themselves as *Arya* (noble) and to the first group they called as *Dasa* (slave). The detailed story of these two hostile groups is found in the ancient written source namely Rigveda (around 1500 BC). It is in the Rigveda, we find the first reference to this social order, with which we are concerned here. According to Rigveda this order, each part of the human society was formed out of the body of the Creator God called *Brahma*. Therefore it has a divine origin. A verse from a hymn of the Rigveda, which deals with this part of the story of this order, reads as: "The *Brahman* (priests) was his mouth, of both his arms was the *Rajanya* (*Kshatriya*, Warriors). His thighs became the *Vaishya* (traders), from his feet the *Sudra* (serving caste) was produced".[9]

This last sentence is widely quoted to emphasize the supposed Divine origins of the caste system. Though the *varna* system, as it came to be called, was encoded much later, as we shall see, it is its extent and power that is the issue here. Positively it gives a definite place in the social order. The Brahmins are the priestly caste – although now their number is declining. The Kshatriya are the warrior caste: of course, there are many regional variations. In Rajasthan the Rajputs, a so-called 'up-and-coming caste', are the dominant caste, a warrior caste but with the status and power of Brahmin. The *Vaishyas* are traders – Gandhi belonged to this caste – and the *sudras* are responsible for all kinds of service work. Yet they are still within the caste system, a status denied the Dalits and tribal people.

In brief, caste – and all the hundreds of sub-castes – controls the type of work a person may do, the rules of inter-dining (or with whom one is allowed to eat), access to water sources especially wells, and most importantly, caste governs extremely strictly who one is allowed to marry. Some deem this, the control of marriages within and between castes, to be the rigid core of the caste system.

Dalits are forced to live in colonies at the edge or outside villages, and in city slums. This creates a huge barrier to social mobility. Dalits cannot drink from the same tea-glasses at tea (chai) shops: the Dalit cup is hidden under the counter. (This practice can be

9. Ralph T.H. Griffith, *The Hymns of the Rigveda* (Delhi: Motilal Banarssidas, 1986 [reprinted]), p. 603.

difficult for a foreigner to notice). Dalit schoolchildren may not drink from the same water pot as caste children. Dalit bridegrooms are often forbidden from riding the traditional horse to the marriage ceremony. Dalits are assigned not only the lowest kinds of tasks, such as street-sweeping, flaying the carcasses of dead animals, but the humiliating job of what is euphemistically called scavenging, but is actually 'removing the night soil' (excrement) from dry toilets, often with bare hands – and mostly this task falls to women.[10]

Types of Violence against Dalits

It is estimated that in India today one in twenty five people suffers caste discrimination on the basis of their work, their blood line or their religion.[11]

According to one estimate, every two hours a Dalit is assaulted, every day three Dalit women are raped, two Dalits are murdered and two Dalit houses are burned.[12] Between 25 and 60 m people in India are bonded labourers and the majority of these are Dalits. The report, *Untouchability in Rural India* (2006) stated that:

- Public Health workers refused to visit Dalit homes in 33 percent of villages.
- Dalits were prevented from entering police stations in 27.6 percent of villages.
- Dalit children had to sit separately while eating in 37.8 percent of government schools.
- Dalits didn't get mail delivered to their homes in 23.5 percent of villages.
- Dalits were denied access to water sources in 48.4 percent of villages because of segregation and untouchability practices.
- Literacy rates for Dalit women are as low as 37.8 percent in rural India.[13]

In some project areas of *Wells for India* the literacy rate of women is nil. Figures here are tricky – some estimates I have read state that Dalit women are 99 percent illiterate. We must also factor in that there are regional variations: as I will discuss, there are

10. Again, this will be discussed later.
11. Mason-John, *Broken Voices*, p. 13.
12. *Combating Caste*, cited in Mason-John, *Broken Voices*, p. 13.
13. Mason-John, *Broken Voices*, p. 14.

indications that the north is more socially backward and therefore a Dalit woman finds it more difficult to cope with the forces ranged against her.

Numerous tragedies and atrocities have occurred if Dalits attempt to marry a caste-person. There is opposition both from Dalit and caste communities. Inter-caste marriages remain one of the greatest taboos in India. Readers will see that the rigidified institution of marriage can be the cause of one of the most miserable and overwhelming experiences of oppression for a Dalit woman.

Globalization

Violence against Dalits has to be put in a wider context. Given that India is now a powerful economic player on the world scene, in addition to the many types of discrimination, the structural effects of the economics of global capitalism are affecting the situation of Dalits in a damaging way. This is due to many factors: for example, the lack of implementation of laws that could improve the lot of Dalit people, government economic policies that encourage large grants from the World Bank, the IMF and large corporations, with scant regard for the consequences for the poorest people, the privatization of forest resources and projects for the beautification of the city that remove the informal sector of employment on which Dalit women and men depend to an enormous extent, since they are so often excluded from formal paid employment. This forces their evacuation to the suburbs where there is little or no employment – all these factors have a worsening effect. They particularly affect women, who are the first to lose jobs in factories. What this means in times of global recession, such as at the present, can only be guessed at. This is how Rajni Tilak, Dalit woman activist and writer, expresses the situation:

> How can the new economic policies help the Dalits? The shrinking government and public sector has already hit them. Will the private companies or multinationals reserve jobs for Dalits? In the villages, their traditional occupations are under threat. I don't understand how people conclude that economic liberalisation will help liberate Dalits. Today, our economic sovereignty is under threat. The multinationals are coming and they will rule the country through the local ruling elite. None of them will offer jobs to Dalits. Another important point to mention is that the education sector is going to be costlier. Where will the poor

Dalit, the agricultural labourer and the landless worker send his children if government schools are closed? Even the middle classes will find it difficult to work. There is no health security. Government hospitals are poor, yet they used to provide some service. Today the concept of the welfare state is considered outdated, but can we do justice to Dalits without a welfare state? How can anyone supporting the New Economic Policies be a supporter of the Dalit cause? Dalits are getting more marginalised in the new pattern of things and we must expose and oppose them vociferously.[14]

This is without mentioning the evictions of thousands of tribal people – Adivasis – consequent on the Sardar Sarovar Dam schemes on the Narmada river. Global capitalism, with the market as its god, and the accompanying idolatry of money and profit, is ruthless in literally sweeping out of its way any section of the population that is unable to be a devotee of the new religion.[15] In capitalism's dominating character – for, as the Latin American theologian Iulio de Santa Ana says, capitalism aims to subordinate every other interest and is deliberate, systemic, hierarchical and patriarchal – it is this last feature, patriarchy, which is closely linked with the lost connections with nature. Hence we will see that because Dalit women in particular are so closely linked with the environment and dependent on its resources, global capitalism has disastrous consequences for their lives. The worsening plight of Dalits within the market system, which replaces the public sector by privatization, is paralleled by the situation of some of the poorest people in many countries, a fact witnessed to by the World Social Forum's slogan '*Another World is possible*'. Dalit activists are prominent at these gatherings, joining many vocal alliances of social movements which are all working for the transformation of the global economic system.

Such gatherings do indicate a positive side of globalization in enabling Dalit groups to come together and organize effective resistance and protest, to meet each other and even to enjoy a celebration of their own culture.

14. Rajni Tilak, 'Dalit Women's Empowerment', Interview, November 2008. www.iheu.org/trackback/3327
15. See M. Grey, *Sacred Longings: Ecofeminist Theology and Globalisation* (London: SCM Press, 2003, Fortress Press, 2004).

Why the Specific Focus on Dalit Women?

Why is it necessary to highlight the plight of Dalit women as such, when the Dalit people as a whole are so clearly discriminated against? The argument here is that the lives of Dalit women experience caste discrimination in a more damaging way than Dalit men. And this has often been a hidden factor in studies of Dalit communities. So here attempts are made to open up in a general way some of the key areas that will be developed later in more detail.

Given the statistics mentioned earlier, the 300m Dalits in India,[16] among these, women – almost 50 percent of the total and 16.3 percent of the total female population of the country, according to the 1991 census – are commonly referred to as 'the least among the Dalits,' 'the Dalits of the Dalits,' or 'thrice Dalits,' – the term was invented by a prominent Dalit woman activist, Ruth Manorama (now internationally respected) – since they suffer discrimination through caste, class and gender. Specifically, they are discriminated against for being female, within their own family and marriage, even by their husbands who frequently beat them and allow them to bear an unequal burden of work, as well as being discriminated against by high-caste people, and third, they are oppressed simply for being Dalit – by the entire caste-system as a whole.

Information on the true situation of Dalit women is far from easy to find. They are ignored by many who write about the oppression of Dalits, subsumed within the generic categories – as I was shocked to discover. Even well-meaning and informed scholars miss the impact of what they have found out. For example, Robert Deliège, in a recent book, *The Untouchables of India*, says this about the work of women:

> The women work as hard as the men, without counting the household chores, which they must do as well.[17]

But it is precisely by factoring in the household chores – including the daily weary search for water, firewood and animal fodder –

16. The document *Dalits and Development Aid* (VODI 2003), p. 16, 5.1 gives the figure as 300m, or 30 percent of the total population, of which 90 percent are below the poverty line. That means 270m people.

17. Robert Deliège, *The Untouchables of India* (trans. Nora Scott; Oxford: Berg, 1999). Originally *Les Untouchables en Inde: Des Castes d'Exclus* (Paris: Editions Imago, 1995), p. 129.

that one can gain some picture of the truth of the lives of Dalit women! Some researchers say that the story behind the story is even harder to tease out. Dr Vimal Thorat (Assistant Professor in Hindi at Indhira Gandhi Open University in New Delhi) claims that Dalit women have been left behind by both the Dalit Movement and the Women's Movement.[18] Even though India now has two generations of articulate, committed Dalit women professionals who are lecturers, professors, activists, (and politicians) he says, their articulation threatens the Dalit male leadership. They will find no place on their committees since their presence itself will be a threat to articulations that refuse to address the issue of brutal violence against Dalit women, gender violence, and nuts and bolts issues like the right to water and a life of dignity. We will need to revisit this failure of the Women's Movement to address Dalit issues. The tensions faced by Dalit women are evocatively expressed by the Dalit poet Taressama:

> We go to work for we are poor
> But the same silken beds mock us
> While we are ravished in broad day light
> Ill-starred our horoscopes are.
> Even our tottering husbands
> Lying on the cots in the corner
> Hiss and shout for revenge
> If we cannot stand their touch.[19]

More than 40 years after the beginning of the political Dalit Movement, it is time to ask, what changes have been achieved for Dalit women? Without denying for a minute that there have been some changes and improvements – notable women activists and leaders, a Dalit political party, some key NGOs – which will be discussed – the question remains: *what is blocking social change? Why is there still such an intolerable level of discrimination in a country that outlawed Untouchability in 1950? What are the gender-specific, underlying structural inhibiting factors that continue to block the transformation of women's lives?* I will now briefly look at a few key areas.

18. Vimal Thorat, 'Dalit Women Today' in *Communalism Combat*, May 2001, Cover story.
19. Cited by Gabriele Dietrich, 'The Relationship between Women's Movement and Dalit Movements: Case Study and Conceptual Analysis', in Gabriele Dietrich, *A New Thing on Earth: Hopes and Fears Facing Feminist Theology* (Delhi: ISPK for TTS, Madurai, 2001), p. 216.

Literacy

With the accusation of Vimal Thorat, we have begun to express the specificity of the situation of Dalit women, this book's focus. Within Dalit women's groups, 90 percent are poor rural women and these are the most disadvantaged of all, with least possibility for education and literacy, more daily struggles for sheer survival – as I have seen each year in Rajasthan. To give one example, the official figures for female Scheduled Caste literacy rates in the four poorest states of India in 1989–1990, (Bihar, Madhya Pradesh, Uttar Pradesh and Rajasthan) give figures of under 2 percent in all areas. In Rajasthan, easily the worst, the figure drops to 0.51 percent in the poorest areas. (This happens to be the Barmer district where *Wells for India* operates through *Gravis* regional Field Centres. Indian economist, Amartya Sen, believes Barmer is the poorest place in the world, on all poverty indicators).

What is an even more depressing statistic is a recent study of the Bhangi caste in Rajasthan. The Bhangi caste – the word Bhanghi refers to their occupational status – ranks very low in the caste hierarchy, and these people experience enormous problems in rising up from this low position. The Bhangis have traditionally been engaged in night scavenging – that is, clearing away human excrement for private houses – and removing the skins of dead animals. Both men and women have had to endure the severe social stigma accompanying this work. In 1961, the female literacy of the Bhangis of Rajasthan was 1.5 percent and in 1981, it had moved only to 3.92 percent. So, when India as a whole was experiencing a rise in literacy, the women of the Bhangi caste in Rajasthan only made a 2 percent gain.[20] On a national level, with Kerala being a notable exception, female literacy compared with boys still remains low in rural areas especially, with the gap widening between Dalit and caste girl children. In Kerala there is a literacy rate of 74 percent – and steadily rising – compared with 7 percent in Bihar.

Yet, if poor rural Dalit women experience huge difficulties in gaining access to education, it is not vastly different in the cities: again, another survey in the city of Jaipur (in 1996) tells of a colony of Dalit people where from 700 families only three children went to

20. S.K. Singh, *Dalit Women – Socio-economic Status and Issues* (Lucknow: New Royal Book Co., 2000), pp. 36–37. The sources for the statistics are National Commission for Women, Government of India, Delhi, 1998.

school. The reasons why access by girls to education is so difficult is a critical issue needing further examination: many of the gender discrimination factors are here shared by the girl-child within the caste system.

My first focus has been literacy, in order to alert attention to the special difficulties of Dalit women in improving their situation compared with other girl children within the caste system. If she is not literate, a Dalit woman may remain ignorant of the social benefits of the reservation policies open to her. She may never gain access to other forms of literacy – knowledge of economic and human rights, and information crucial for health and nutrition. My experience recently in rural Rajasthan is that *some* women are awakening to the need for literacy and are very enthusiastic that their girl children should have access to education. Yet many are so bowed down with the drudgery of their lives that they cannot envision that it could be different. Many rural villages are so remote that access to schools is almost impossible and the bias against girl education so strong that it still functions as a glass ceiling. The burden for rural women in these areas is made worse by the need for men to migrate for wage labour (if agriculture fails) so the responsibility to keep the community going falls solely to women. Survival is often the only goal.

Work

The issue of women's work is also critical and needs special attention. Here there is a particular difference between Dalit and Hindu women within the caste system. Dalit women through sheer necessity are more likely to be in paid employment and can seem to caste women to enjoy a relative freedom in this respect as well as a sense of pride as being wage earners. (It is so well-documented that Hindu Brahmin women endure severe restriction of movement as not to need repetition here).[21] But this superficial freedom is easily romanticized: it conceals the truth that Dalit women are far less in paid employment than their men-folk and earn lower wages

21. See Rama Mehta, *Inside the Haveli* (London/Delhi: Penguin, 1994). Here a young couple fall in love at the University of Bombay (Mumbai). The young bride is brought home to a haveli in the ancient city of Udaipur, where she is forced to live in purdah – extreme seclusion - and scarcely ever leaves the family household.

than men for the same work. There are few opportunities for promotion in the workplace – preference is always for men. In many rural situations when men move on to better paid factory work for even the civil service, it will be women who take responsibility for agriculture. Women are frequently in a position where they are forced to spend more than they earn and are therefore constantly in debt and thus prey to the ever-present money-lender. Scant attention is given to the fact that Dalit women endure a range of sexual harassments in the workplace – an issue demanding further attention.

Political Representation

Despite certain political opportunities Dalit women are under-represented in government and the decision-making process – and of course, Christian Dalit women do not enjoy the opportunities that reservation policies offer to their Hindu counterparts. In 2003, less than 8 percent of parliamentary seats and less than 6 percent of cabinet positions and 4 percent of positions in the High Court and Supreme Court were filled by women. There is a Dalit political party, the Bahujan Samaj Party, and it has recently been led by a woman, Mayawati, Chief Minister of Uttar Pradesh. In the recent national election it was even rumoured that she might become Prime Minister. But this has made little impact on the ground realities for Dalit women and men: sadly, the temptations of power have frequently led to corruption.

So even if my focus is more on poor, rural Dalit women, obstacles remain even for educated Dalit women in employment, wages, appointments, promotion, political representation and personal relations.[22] Through the government reservation policies the major beneficiaries for Scheduled Tribes and Castes are, unsurprisingly, men:

> Further, as a result of persistent casteism and corruption, many seats in colleges and positions in government reserved for Scheduled Castes and Scheduled tribes go unfilled, though qualified Dalit candidates do apply. Thus, if a qualified

22. Moses Seenarine, *Dalit Women: Victims or Beneficiaries of Affirmative Action Policies in India – A Case Study*, Brown Bag Lecture, S. Asian Institute, Columbia University, 10 April 1996, pp. 1–12.

Dalit woman applies for a job or college seat reserved for an
SC/ST, she is told to apply as a woman; if she applied for a job
or college seat reserved for women, she is told to apply as an
SC/ST.[23]

All sources express the painful truth that Dalit women suffer
from multiple discriminations of class, caste, gender and cultural
traditions, at every level of society – village, district, state and
nationally – as well as in their own homes and most intimate
relations. Within this general picture widows are the most vulnerable
and open to the greatest exploitation.

Health

When it comes to health, many Dalit women are anaemic and
undernourished, suffering also from tuberculosis, eye problems and
problems of pregnancy, post-delivery complications and maternal
mortality. In our project areas of Rajasthan, these conditions affect
all rural women. Scheduled Caste women are also prone to
occupational health problems – through the lifting of heavy weights
and contact with hazardous material. In the drought situation in
Rajasthan, where our project partners operated Food for Work
programmes, it was noticeable that it was the women who took on
the heavy work of deepening ponds – in addition to the usual
burdens of child care and the search for water, wood and fodder.
As I write (in 2009) there is a new Government Employment Scheme,
where every person who registers is entitled to a hundred days'
paid work: for women what this means is the backbreaking task of
wielding pick-axes in building new roads. (This may not even be
rationally worked out – the roads may be washed away as soon as
the monsoon rains arrive).

Internalization of Oppression

In this brief introduction I have alluded to the fact that very little
social change has been achieved by Dalit women and asked what
the inhibiting factors are. One of the most deep-seated problems in
the internalization of the social situation. This has many expressions
and many different levels of severity. In its broadest frame of

23. Seenarine, *Dalit Women.*

reference it can be connected with the stigma of being female, and therefore 'the second sex', inferior to the male subject in law and in religion. Discrimination against the girl-child is still rife in contemporary India. Abortions of the girl-child are still on the increase especially in middle-class urban India, due to the availability of amniocentesis, and the regarding of girl children as burdens in a culture where wealth acquisition is paramount.

Centuries of being bought in marriage and being on the receiving end of sexual discrimination and abuse have left deep psychic wounds. And these wounds are shared with many women in poor countries who have never had access to a life of dignity.

But the second frame of reference is to racist discrimination and here Dalit women share some of the injustices of Afro-American women who, descendants of African slaves, suffer both from poverty and racial discrimination, never allowed to forget a background of slavery even in contemporary America. So Alice Walker coined the term 'womanist' for African-American women to be more radical than 'feminist'. (And it is true that these terms have been used divisively to dismiss feminism as Western and foreign, and to divide women into 'good' and 'bad'). Womanist theology has had a distinctive development in the USA and been influenced by the biblical figure of the Egyptian slave woman Hagar in her relationship with her mistress, Sarah.[24] Valerie Mason John in her research on Dalit women, (referred to earlier), herself an African American, found herself frequently considered as a Dalit woman. Sometimes when travelling on a bus she would be shouted at as 'Coolie'! or 'Porter!' and told to get off the bus and load the luggage. Even a young friend in India once surprised her by saying that even if she had a dark skin, she had a pure heart![25]

The womanist/feminist tension is reflected in India by the fact that, as Gabriele Dietrich, feminist theologian and social activist in Tamil Nadu describes:

> while Dalit women have had to battle hard to achieve a clear perception of their concerns in the "mainstream" Women's Movement in India, they have also found it difficult to build fronts in Dalit Movements and have sometimes needed support

24. See Dolores Williams, *Sisters in the Wilderness, The Challenge of Womanist Godtalk* (Maryknoll, NY: Orbis Books, 1993).
25. Mason-John, *Broken Voices*, pp. xiii–xiv.

from "autonomous" Women's Movement to build their organisations.[26]

Dietrich argues strongly that Dalit women should resist polarizing women against each other: rather, Dalit women and Dalit Movements

> can make a decisive impact on the Women's Movement and class movements as a whole. It is possible to come to a conceptual understanding in which womanist and feminist can be used virtually synonymously, provided the Women's Movement consistently stands up against casteism and untouchability.[27]

Third, this tension with the Women's Movement as a whole highlights that Dalit women suffer in a uniquely distinctive way. The legacy of colonialism, together with the stigma of untouchability have affected women in a far more humiliating way than men – for example, in some areas, in not being allowed to cover their breasts, or wear the breast cloth. Of course this has to be put in the historical context of numerous dress restrictions for Untouchables.[28] The fact that in the past Untouchables had been forced to wear a piece of clothing until it fell to pieces, together with the difficulty of finding water, meant that they were frequently dirty and smelt badly. This in turn contributed to the internalization of inferiority and social stigma. Even if some high-caste women had been traditionally bare-breasted, the right to cover the breast is symbolic of female dignity – as it was with men's right to wear a shirt. Although as early as 1812 Colonel Munro, the British Resident of Travancore (South Kerala) decreed that Christian women should be allowed to over their breasts, this was resisted by the Travancore Government. In general the missionaries continued to protest against this restriction. But as late as 1930/1931 in a dispute between the Kallars of Ramnad district, the Kallars recalled eight prohibitions against Untouchables, including that women were not allowed to cover the upper part of the body.

This internalization of social stigma – which has been observed by the Women's Movement globally – is an especially harsh obstacle

26. Gabriele Dietrich, 'Subversion, Transgression, Transcendence: "Asian Spirituality" in the Light of Dalit and Adivasi Struggles' in Gabriele Dietrich, *A New Thing on Earth: Hopes and Fears Facing Feminist Theology* (Delhi: ISPCK for TTS, Madurai, 2001): pp. 238–50, quotation pp. 243–44.

27. Dietrich, 'Subversion, Transgression, Transcendence', p. 244.

28. Deliège, *The Untouchables of India*, pp. 107–108.

when combined with all the factors just discussed. It can be observed in a range of expressions – from apathy, to a severe fatalism and cringing subservience. What I hope to focus on is the way that some women have broken out of this and become leaders in their communities.

The Women's Movement and Dalit Women

There are two main problems concerning the tensions between the Feminist Movement and Dalit women which have already been referred to. According to Gabriele Dietrich, there is a tendency to assimilate and identify the problem of Dalit women with the problems of all caste Hindu women. Although these are serious – and many injustices like female infanticide, domestic violence, child marriage, dowry, cruelty of mothers-in-law, problems of widows, crippling work load, poverty and health, are common to most Indian women (especially in a rural situation) to assume that patriarchy is the cause of all of these is to hide the specificity of caste issues and caste oppression for Dalit women.[29] The truth needs to be sought at the point of origin of the caste system: we need to explore the way patriarchy has become intrinsically interwoven with it. Issues of purity, the stigma of pollution, prohibitions on inter-dining and the exclusivity of the marriage circle are all part of this picture, and are all factors maintained at the expense of stigmatizing of the Dalit woman.

Second, there is what one writer calls the 'aggressive wing' of the Feminist Movement that can be problematic, since it:

> often denies the compensatory satisfaction women derive through practising the virtues of service and self-sacrifice. And the traditionalists tend to deny women a life independent of the traditional roles she is expected to play. However, when one gets down to the individual, one often finds that she wants both.[30]

The rejection of the model of the self-sacrificing wife, an image largely rejected by contemporary European and North American feminism (and frequently declared a bone of contention in the face

29. Dietrich, 'The Relationship between Women's Movement and Dalit Movements', in Dietrich, *A New Thing on Earth*, pp. 203–27.
30. Sumitra Bhave, *Pan on Fire: 8 Dalit Women Tell their Stories* (New Delhi: Indian Social Institute, 1988).

of assumptions of traditional Christianity) may fail to grasp the total reality of the Dalit woman and how she negotiates her areas of freedom and moments of joy. Yet the precise way that patriarchy permeates the way caste operates negatively and differently for *both* Hindu and Dalit women is a crucial issue and has to be addressed to find a way forward.

We need to understand precisely how the intersection of the caste system with patriarchy, plus the misunderstandings and discrimination from both the Feminist Movement and Dalit Movement as a whole – already referred to – are all factors contributing to the burden of suffering and injustice of the lives of Dalit women. This is not in any way to reduce Dalit women to the level of victim, even if she is a daily victim of many sorts of violence. I hope to highlight some of the many remarkable stories of resistance, transgression, courage and hope in a changing situation.

In conclusion, this has been a Chapter opening up some of the problematic areas in the lives of Dalit people in general and women in particular. All these issues need exploring in greater depth, and this will be the focus of the next chapter.

Chapter 2

Born a Woman, Born a Dalit: The Poisoned Chalice – the Daily Lives of Dalit Women

Daylight would die. Darkness would reign.
We are at our hut's door. No single light inside.
Lights burning in houses around.
Kitchen fires too. *Bhakris* beaten out.
Vegetables, gruels cooked.
In our nostrils, the smell of food. In our stomachs darkness.
From our eyes, welling up, streams of tears.
Slicing darkness, a shadow heavily draws near.
On head, a burden. Her legs a – t-totter.
Thin, dark body … my mother.
All days she combs the forest for firewood.
We await her return.[1]

This heartrending poem of the hungry child desperately awaiting his mother's return from the forest is made even more poignant by the fact that the poem goes on to recount how one day, his mother was bitten by a snake in the forest and dies. The child's eyes never stop seeking his mother. How can the Dalit child survive without the long daily labour of the mother? The fate of the mother has direct consequences for the child's very survival.

Chapter 1 highlighted specific areas in the lives of Dalit people and of women specifically, especially areas where the type and level of discrimination was different from that against women within the caste system. It also placed this discrimination in the wider context of the Women's Movement in India. Now Chapter 2 deepens the picture, exploring certain key areas, always trying to understand how discrimination against Dalits in general targets women specifically, and how their reality differs from that of women within

1. Waman Nibalkar, 'Mother', in Arjun Dangle (ed.), *Poisoned Bread: Translations from Modern Marathi Dalit Literature* (Hyderabad: Orient Longman, 1992), this poem translated by Priya Adarkar.

the caste system, given that discrimination against caste women is also widespread, and that poverty is the defining context.

The Long Drawn-out Daily Toil

Burnad Fatima, President of the Tamil Nadu Women's Forum (herself a Dalit) spoke movingly in 2002 at the United Nations Committee on the Elimination of Racial Discrimination in Geneva, of the unremittingly hard work of Dalit women.[2] She described the drudgery of rural Dalit women in the fields, work for which they earn less than 1 US dollar a day. This is in addition to unpaid domestic work. In a working day that can last between 17 and 24 hours, Dalit women do all kinds of menial work: as well as agricultural work, they are occupied in casual labour in road construction, laying tar in the hot sun often without sandals, or working in brick kilns, or breaking stones, or manual scavenging – which means handling and disposing of human excrement – as well as cleaning sewage and sweeping roads. Their daily chores include long journeys for water, food and fodder, journeys which make them constantly vulnerable to sexual harassment. This vulnerability is worsened when Dalit women in the cities are forced to work late shifts in factories, and may be treated as prostitutes.

In a shocking statistic, Burnad Fatima showed how Dalit women work harder than both bullocks and men. Bullocks and men work in a hectare (2 acres) in a year for 1,064 and 1,202 hours respectively, and women for more than 3,485 hours. What this means in terms of weariness, stress, hunger and sickness can only be left to the imagination. This underlying fact of the lives of Dalit women is one reason why it is difficult for them to attend protest meetings and action for social change. The struggle for survival simply dominates existence.

Some real life stories illustrate this. This next is a story from a Dalit man, Muli, from the Bauri caste, living in a small village, Kapilesawar, three miles from Bhubaneswar, the capital of Orissa. It tells of his wife, Kia: theirs was a loveless marriage and Muli frequently deserted his wife to run off with prostitutes for whom he acted as a pimp. This is how he describes her:

2. Speech of Burnad Fatima, CERD: Geneva, 8–9 August 2002.

My wife is a hard worker, and certainly much stronger than I am. She usually earns more than I do. She cuts paddy faster and better than most men, and hardly anyone can keep up with her when she works in road construction gangs. She doesn't like eating unless she has earned a wage. She becomes impatient when she has to spend time idly.[3]

We will return later to the struggles of Kia's life, one of unremitting drudgery. This is certainly the same picture of women's work we perceive in rural Rajasthan. In times of drought, if agriculture fails, the men have no work, and either migrate to the cities in search of it, or are forced to be idle, where they frequently succumb to opium or alcohol addiction. (This is frequently alluded to as a huge social problem at Women's Meetings). But women struggle on to feed their children, keep the family going and to care for the elderly, a responsibility made almost impossible if their husbands spend the money on alcohol or drugs – a fact reoccurring in many contexts. Yet, on the other hand, in the context of the extended family there is a sense that women negotiate how much work they will do, even if the freedom to do so is limited. Dalit women have a tremendous pride in their work, especially if this is paid work. They want the option of paid work rather then spending the day in housework and have a strong sense of the contribution their work makes. The writers of *The Silken Swing*, a study of three different Dalit caste groups in Gujurat (the Vankars and Bhangi communities of Varasada village, and the Koli-Patel communities of Gamph village in Dandhuka)[4] discovered this:

> Even if men dismiss women's labour as inconsequential, the women have a clear sense of achievement regarding their work. They also feel and say, that their work is better than the men's.

This important point will need to be stressed in conclusion, as it is clearly not the issue of hard work that is a cause of resentment and resistance, but the injustice of the conditions within which Dalit women have to work. There are also attempts to resist the dependency on caste people. For example, the women of Gudaliya, a village 125 kms from Jaipur, in a study on *Dalit Women in Rajasthan*,

---

3. James Freeman, *Untouchable: An Indian Life History* (Stanford, CA: Stanford University Press, 1979), p. 257.

4. Fernando Franco, Jyotsan Macwan, Suguna Ramanathan (eds), *The Silken Swing: The Cultural Universe of Dalit Women* (Calcutta: Stree, 2000), p. 89.

told that they were proud of the fact that they had refused food and buttermilk from upper-caste people. This act had caused tensions with the upper-caste, because of their belief that giving buttermilk to the Raigars is an act of *dharma* (a good act) – perhaps similar to the Christian belief that acts of charity are meritorious.[5]

Another woman, Laddo Koli, from Kacchi Basti, a resettlement colony on the outskirts of Jaipur city tells how she has three children, is illiterate, and unable to educate any of her children. Her husband earns about 1,500 rupees per month as a construction worker (about £25), but gives her no money, is alcoholic and abusive. Forced to work simply to feed herself and children she earns about 900–1,000 rupees per month (under £15) at a nearby *mandi* (wholesale market) carrying heavy bundles on her head. She neither has a ration card nor knows how to get one, has no water, but pays 50 rupees a month to a neighbour to use hers. Her entire income is spent on surviving, yet she can neither afford vegetables nor to send her children to school.[6] Her story illustrates the ever-present problem of accessing even what rights are available to Dalits by state, national and international law. (A summary of these rights is given in Appendix B).

In an urban context the work of Dalit women has been seriously affected – as mentioned – by slum clearance, partly consequent on World Bank funding. Sweeping and cleaning jobs – considered polluted tasks – are now in danger of being steadily privatized, and Dalit women will again be the first victims of job loss. One of the difficulties of Dalit women getting access to education and to their legal rights are the difficult conditions of life in the slums. As one woman relates:

> I was born 30 years ago in the slums of a major city of Maharashtra. The slums were beside the railways and were full of huts made of straw and dung and small houses made of corrugated iron. They were in rows and when you stepped out you were almost in someone else's home. There was no drainage and no fresh water, and there were only four public toilets for a community of

5. The Programme on Women's Economic, Social and Cultural Rights (PWESCR) together with the Centre for Dalit Rights, Jaipur, *Dalit Women in Rajasthan: Status of Economic, Social and Cultural Rights, A Study* (New Delhi: PWESCR, 2007).
6. This is paraphrased from PWESCR: *Dalit Women in Rajasthan*, p. 19.

three thousand families or more. That meant that people went to the toilet on the streets and on the edge of the slums.[7]

As girls reach puberty, the lack of privacy for washing again makes them vulnerable to sexual harassment. Lack of toilet facilities at home and the fact that frequently toilet facilities were non-existent and the street was the only solution, meant that women would only be able to go to the toilet after dark. All of this hinders access to meaningful work, education and medical care. Lack of funds to pay for medical care may mean reliance on traditional – even superstitious – practices, often with fatal results. Activist Ruth Manorama highlights many health problems of Dalit women:

- The sex ratio of females in every thousand of males has declined from 957 in 1961 to 922 1999.
- Women take nutrient deficient food since most of them are below the poverty line (a district level study in Maharastra).
- Around 56 percent of Dalit Women suffer from some form of anaemia, as compared to 49.1 percent of non-SC/ST women. Similarly a much higher percentage of Dalit Women are under-nourished as compared to their non-SC/ST female counterparts according to the second National Family Health Survey, 1998–99).
- With significant cuts in government expenditure for public health services, on which the majority of Dalit women continue to rely, and commercialization and privatization of public healthcare services, poor Dalit women are being forced to fend for themselves either to live with ill-health or to enter into health-related debt. This has the chain effect of affecting the health status of Dalit children and their families, besides lowering the income generating capacity of Dalit women.[8]

Dalit Women and the Environment: Access to Water and Land

Farming, agriculture are in your hands, but is the land in your hands? No caste, religion or class gives land into women's hands.[9]

7. Valerie Mason-John *Broken Voices: Untouchable Women Speak Out* (New Delhi: India Research Press, 2008), pp. 124–26.

8. Dr Ruth Manorama, *Dalit Women: Downtrodden of the Downtrodden*, India Together, 24 February 2006.

9. Cited in Hugo Gorringe, *Untouchable Citizens* (New Delhi: Sage Publications, 2005), Chapter 6, 'Dalit Women and Dalit Movements', p. 227.

Access to water, food security and land is supposed to be enshrined in India's constitution, yet, as has already been hinted, these areas represent points of acute suffering and oppression Dalit women's unique situation as regards closeness to natural resources and organic life in both city and village, has failed to raise global awareness, both of the negative aspects as an area of great suffering for women, and of the positive aspects, namely that they possess wisdom, skills and initiatives that are seldom acknowledged. Many questions need to be highlighted.

First, given the high population of Indian people in the villages, the daily lives of Dalit women are focused on the daily search for water, fuel and fodder: but the search for water is fraught with danger as access to the wells of caste-people is forbidden. Countless stories of violence, beatings and rape, even murder are too numerous to recount. I will tell two, a negative one – sadly, more common – and a positive story. Luke Harding, a *Guardian* reporter, relates the story of Ms. Devi who told that when she drew water from the upper-caste well, some thugs beat her 11 year-old daughter unconscious. When she went to the Police station to complain, she was thrown out and called a 'whore'. A gang of upper-caste locals then sexually assaulted her in her hut that night.[10] (We will need to return to the role of police in the oppression of Dalit women). The Dalit Centre for Human Rights (DCR) in Jaipur, in conjunction with the International Movement for Dalit rights, exists to fight such cases.

A similar story with a happier ending was told to me by a friend, an educated Dalit woman, now living in Britain. Growing up in a village in Tamil Nadu where her father was a teacher in a caste school, she, the young daughter, had to fetch water from the Dalit well, a long way away, which always meant a degree of danger from harassment. One day an upper-caste boy threw a snake down the Dalit well, so as to deliberately pollute it. She then decided to draw water from the caste well and immediately there was protest from upper-caste women who tried to prevent her. She persisted and a large delegation confronted her father with the 'offence' of his daughter. Her father held his ground, supported her action, and threatened that the entire community would draw water from

10. Luke Harding, 'Sex Hell of Dalit Women Exposed', *The Guardian*. New Delhi, 9 May 2001.

the upper-caste well until their own well was purified.[11] The Dalit well was cleaned up in double-quick time! But the politics of the access question have still not been tackled.

The second story witnesses to the immense courage and strength of Dalit women in the face of oppression. Gabriele Dietrich, cited in Chapter 1, tells of a water struggle of Telengana in the state of Andhra Pradesh.[12] This is an important story as it shows the strength of Dalit women as social activists – where they can overcome the obstacles to mobilize for social change. Telengana is an area which ought to have abundant water, but because of unsustainable politics of canal building, and a steady increase in water hungry cash crops – chillies, cotton, sunflower rather than dry crops like jowar and basra – has now become drought-prone. The struggle was carried about by an NGO called Jabasadhana Samiti (JSI) around the Srisailan Canal. There were many non-violent demonstrations – or *satyagrahas*.[13] Six lakhs[14] signatures were collected and sent to the President of India. These expressly excluded males between 18–55 years as the women felt this age-group were responsible for the mal-development. This is a long story, and caste politics makes it complex. But it was largely the efforts of Dalits, women and children who were successful in keeping the Canal issue on the agenda and witnesses to the knowledge and wisdom of Dalit women as to the crucial significance of good water management.

This story is paralleled by other land-related struggles in contexts of the growth of agro-businesses on a national scale. Dalits – as has been explained – are largely landless (frequently bonded-labourers, including child labourers) thus dependent on waste-land for grazing. When industries or tree plantation schemes encroach, land gets fenced in, and people cannot graze their goats or again, have access to water points. Yet Gabriele Dietrich gives many examples of Dalits and Adivasis acquiring new skills in regenerating waste-lands, watershed management in Maharashtra, and of Dalit women developing skills in biomass.

11. Personal story from Revd Jasmine Jebakani, Christian Dalit theologian, then based at Sarum College, Salisbury, April 2003.
12. Gabriele Dietrich, 'Dalit Feminism and the Environment,' *In God's Image* 19.3 (Sept 2000), pp. 21–26.
13. *Satyagraha* or non-violent demonstration was one of Gandhi's most important political tools. It now plays a major political role in action to protect the environment.
14. One lakh = 100,000.

I have seen this myself, sitting on top of a loose stone check dam in Rajasthan in the Aravali hills – part of a watershed harvesting scheme to conserve monsoon water – with tribal (Adivasi) women, who wanted us to admire their work, insisting it was their own and not the men-folk's. They dreamt of flattening the hills – thus facilitating access to land. Access to water and land makes the difference between life and death. Trees are also a vital part of this struggle for survival. The women of the Bishnoi tribe of north-western Rajasthan know this all too well. In this area in the Baap district of the Thar Desert they are faithful to the principles given by their god, Jambu, who taught them to honour the trees.

This famous story goes back to the nineteenth century, when a Bishnoi woman, Amrita Devi, was celebrating her marriage, and along came the soldiers of the Maharajah of Jodhpur to chop down the trees to build a palace for their ruler. 'Over our dead bodies!' cried the women and they and their daughters hugged the trees. *Chipko* means tree-hugging. Tragically, the women were all killed – but since the 1970s there is an international Chipko Movement for tree conservation, remembering the courage and the wisdom of Amrita Devi and her companions. In all the *Gravis* Field Centres of the Thar Desert there is a *Chipko* poster on the wall, a constant reminder of their bravery and the importance of trees. I have discovered other contemporary Chipko stories from NGOs who work with Dalit communities to struggle against chopping down trees and to prevent illegal encroachment over common land.

Along with trees goes the importance of seeds: Dalit women are in the forefront of the struggle to conserve seeds, especially in a political climate of patenting traditional crops and trees that are a vital part of their way of life – as Vandana Shiva has demonstrated in her many works. But frequently their efforts are subsumed in the general ecological movements, so that their specific skills and wisdom can go unnoticed.

Dalit Women, even given all the statistics on illiteracy, internalization of social stigma, and the daily struggle against violence, are at the forefront of this land struggle, developing alternative systems, struggling against the injustices of prawn farming in Tamil Nadu and so on. *But now they now need to be recognized as at the forefront in a changed economic context where privatization, new farming techniques and increased mechanization will take away their jobs.*

Dalit Women and Scavenging

Formerly the traditional occupation of the Bhangi people, in some cases the Chamar caste (leatherworkers), I mention this separately as scavenging still represents an acute area of suffering for many Dalit women mostly in an urban context.

> It is estimated that around 1.3 million Dalits in India, mostly women, make their living through manual scavenging – a term used to describe the job of removing human excrement from dry toilets and sewers using basic tools such as thin boards, buckets and baskets, lined with sacking, carried on the head. Manual scavengers earn around 60p per month. Though this vile and inhumane practice was abolished by law in India in 1993,[15] the practice is deeply entrenched in South Asian societies.

> The British created official posts for manual scavengers. All institutions – army, railway, courts, industries and major towns were equipped with dry toilets instead of water-borne sewerage...this is not to say the British invented manual scavenging, rather they intervened to institutionalise it.[16]

The practice has an ancient origin, although the oldest civilization of India, the Harappan, (2500 BCE) possessed waterborne toilets. With the end of this civilization sanitation practice took a downward turn. Manual scavenging is still prevalent across Asia, references indicating that these bucket toilets were also prevalent in Africa, China and Japan, although not necessarily linked with caste.[17] Many factors coalesce to increase the growth of manual scavenging: the lack of control and maintenance of the sewage systems, the growth of housing with no open spaces and development of slums, and even the fact of access to clean water and medicine of the middle classes that allowed them to ignore environmental problems and the resulting diseases.

Over 70m people still use dry latrines and more than 100m Dalits are involved in cleaning them together with other tasks, like handling

15. This Act was called 'The Employment of Manual Scavengers and Construction of Dry Latrines Prohibition' Act. Using or maintaining dry toilets is illegal and liable for punishment with a fine.

16. Gita Ramaswamy, *India Stinking: Manual Scavengers in Andhra Pradesh and Their Work* (New Delhi and Chennai: Navayana, 2005), p. 4. The first paragraph is a précis and forms part of DSN's *Foul Play* publicity against manual scavenging.

17. Ramaswamy, *India Stinking*, p. 5.

solid waste and industrial waste, lifting and flaying fallen carcasses, handling hides and collecting rubbish. Since 1992 the Government of India has been committed to the 'Liberation and Rehabilitation of the Scavengers'. Scavenging involves women as they are mostly responsible for waste from private homes – and men for industrial waste. A study of the Bhangi people in Rajasthan in 1992 (sometimes known as Mehtar) showed that of 2,856 cases, 89 percent were occupied in scavenging. It is an issue for women specifically in this changing context, because where men become more occupationally mobile (with increased opportunities denied to women) they leave behind scavenging and women pick up the shortfall. In Delhi, for example, in three generations of women, occupational mobility had not improved.[18] Practices do vary from caste to caste. The Balmiki, a nomadic caste from Telugu in the south, do not allow their daughters to engage in manual scavenging – only their daughters-in-law. They reckon that because their daughters marry out of the family it will be up to the parents-in-law to make the decision.[19]

Here is how three women from Andhra Pradesh described their work: They used a piece of tin to lift the excrement into a woven basket lined with leaves to prevent leakage and then carried the basket to a place far away where such refuse could be dumped.[20] Today their children and grandchildren are in the same work, even though one of these is highly educated. One of these men can only do the work when high on alcohol, and this is not uncommon among men. One of the women, Kotamma, says the work is only done in the dark: 'Everybody shits: but who wants to see it? So we work at night.' Like the Balmiki, the women do not take their daughters to this work, but only their daughters-in-law. At least let their daughters be free of the practice now, they say.

The same phenomenon is noted by the research of Dr Bindeshwar Pathak, founder of *Sulabh International*, and winner of many awards.[21] He selected three urban habitats from the state of Bihar, Patna, Arrah and Muzaffarpur, and worked with a complex

18. Ramaswamy, *India Stinking*, p. 38.

19. Ramaswamy, *India Stinking*, p. 39.

20. This section is paraphrased from Ramaswamy, *India Stinking*, pp. 32–33.

21. Bindeshwar Pathak, *Road to Freedom: A Sociological Study of the Abolition of Scavenging in India* (New Delhi: Motilal Banarsidass Publishing, 1991). The work was carried out as part of the author's PhD thesis submitted in 1985.

sample of 600 households. His findings are similar to those I have described in areas of education and housing. No person had actually completed schooling and 93.3 percent of women were illiterate. Very few parents sent their girls to school. (We need to remember that attention to the position of women in India nationally only commenced with the Government's Sixth Five Year Plan, 1980–1985).

The only 'positive' area – if it can be called that – was unemployment which hardly existed. But this was because there was no competition for the job of scavenging. When Dr Pathak enquired further he discovered that actually it was the women who were doing the work of scavenging: the men did the socially superior tasks of sweeping.[22] He further discovered that there was a very high rate of smoking among men – and that was shared by women, although the women smoked the cheapest 'bidis' available. There was also a huge problem with alcohol, most of the men confessing themselves to be addicted. But only one woman admitted to drinking. This reinforces the picture where most of the earnings will be spent on cigarettes and alcohol – which is of a cheap and crude variety.

The second issue for women about scavenging is their vulnerability for sexual harassment on the way to and from, or during work. Third, scavenging, over and above any other activity, condemns families to live in a socially and economically discriminated-against situation: their excluded situation makes it very difficult for them to organize politically for change. Pathak found little or no political awareness among the Bhangi people in his study. They were neither aware of their rights under Indian law, nor that the Government had outlawed Untouchability and discriminatory practices. So the work of liberation of *Sulabh International* proved vital for social change. Since the 1970s Sulabh has constructed thousands of Public Toilet Facilities in many states of India. These function also as Health Education Centres and have provided many jobs for former Untouchables. Pathak's study investigates in depth the lives of some of the 'liberated Dalits.' In all cases the 'liberated' scavengers were women: even though their standard of living remained very low, the fact that they were able to leave behind their humiliating work, and take jobs like

22. Pathak, *Road to Freedom*, p. 104.

maidservants and sweepers, had completely changed their lives. A much greater commitment to girl education was observed.

When visiting Sulabh's Headquarters in Delhi in 2001 it was impressive to see their commitment to girl children's education and that women were employed as equals in Sulabh's own staff. Not the least of the achievements was to produce lunch, using as fuel biogas from these Public Facilities! Yet, Sulabh's work is not without its critics. Although Pathak is liberating Dalits from manual scavenging, they are not liberated from caste but only experience it in a new form:

> The Sulabh toilet mirrors the caste system. The caretaker (who does not soil his hands) is usually a caste Hindu ... he is paid a salary between Rs 1,500 and 2,000 per month. The caretaker also collects money from users and supervises the actual cleaners, either Bhangis or Madigas who work a shift system and are paid Rs 600 to Rs 900 per month. The Sulabh endeavour has not been able to break the stranglehold of the caste system on occupations.[23]

But scavenging still continues on a wide scale and it will take more than Sulabh's efforts to eradicate it. Nor was Gandhi any more successful – and we will return to his efforts. Suffice it to say that, although Untouchability was at the heart of Gandhi's ideas of reform, and their plight moved him with genuine compassion, it was reform of caste rather than its eradication that Gandhi sought. Second, he had a tendency to romanticize the position of the Bhangi and her work:

> "The Bhangi", Gandhi wrote, "constitutes the foundation of all services. A Bhangi does for society what a mother does for her baby. A mother washes her baby of the dirt and ensures his health. Even so the Bhangi protects and safeguards the health of the entire community by maintaining sanitation for it".[24]

This romanticization is also seen in his statement that he loved scavenging and that, although he did not believe in rebirth, if he was to be reborn, he would like it to be as an Untouchable. Although in his Ashram, Gandhi insisted on the work of cleaning the toilets being shared, that fact that he called the Dalits 'Harijans' or 'Children of God', a term which can refer to prostitutes, and is regarded as

23. Ramaswamy, *India Stinking*, p. 23.
24. Ramaswamy, *India Stinking*, pp. 18–19.

patronizing, has meant that Dalits do not regard Gandhi as their leader in any way – and for more serious reasons, as we shall see. Both S.K. Singh and Gita Ramaswamy in their books outline the complex political action and reform movements necessary for the removal of these gross injustices – and we shall return to these in the final chapter.[25]

Bonded Labour

It often goes unnoticed that a majority of the poor people locked into debt and bonded labour are Dalit people and this again is another area of suffering for Dalit women. This was a particularly severe situation in the days of the Raj. Anne Grodzins Gold tells the story of the Regar (Chamar) people of Rajasthan. She interviewed Jamuni Regar, an elderly woman, full of memories of the harsh days under the Raj (whom she refers to as *the Court*). She describes the system of bonded labour or 'begār'. The women were called 'begāri-wali' and would be summoned by the king or queen about once every eight days. Their work varied from singing and dancing for 'the Court', to carrying their 'cots' (beds) long distances from the fort to the water reservoir. Sometimes the Regars' own beds would be taken when a large number of guests were expected. There was even a memory of ejecting a woman in childbirth from her bed! The women's special work was to grind the grain for the horses and collect cow dung from 25 cows. This was all very hard work and the greatest area of resentment was that it was unpaid and that the women were beaten if they refused or in any way did not comply with the Court's demands, as the following interview shows:

> Bhoju: What did he give you?
> Jamuni: He gave us nothing at all, it was *begār*, we worked for free…
> Bhoju: Did you take bread?
> Jamuni: No, no bread, no day wages, nothing! … It was only the farmers who gave us grain for repairing their shoes, but from the rulers we got nothing.[26]

25. S.K. Singh *Dalit Women – Socio-economic Status and Issues* (Lucknow: New Royal Book Co., 2000), pp. 140–42.

26. Anne Grodzins Gold and Bhoju Ram Gujar, *In the Time of Trees and Sorrows: Nature, Power and Memory in Rajasthan* (New Delhi: Oxford University Press, 2002), pp. 97–99.

Jamuni considered that it was a time of sorrow and unhappiness under the 'begār' system, which lasted until the death of the *Court* and independence. There are also allusions to sexual exploitation by the Court, but such an area of shame exists around this, that the researchers proceeded with sensitivity and in many cases did not probe the silence of the women. I have witnessed this difficulty myself, so great is the shame around these areas. It is particularly serious in the area of domestic violence, where trying to penetrate the silence may bring a terrible reaction down on the head of the woman or girl concerned.

The moneylender is very active in the rural situation, especially if the harvest fails and there is no money for seeds for the next sowing. (Farmers rely on there being a harvest to save seeds for the following sowing). Rates on interest can be so extortionate that people can be indebted into the next generation. In some of *Wells for India's* projects among tribal people we were told that reliance on the moneylender had decreased: the rate on interest had dropped from 180 percent to 24 percent - a rate that still sounded too high to our ears.

The Marital and Family Situation of Dalit Women

Earlier I drew attention to the fact that, to some degree, Dalit women are less restricted in their daily lives than High-Caste women, whose every movement is governed by some clause in the Code of Manu, rigorously adhered to, at least in traditional circles. I also said that this was a situation easy to romanticize. Whereas the freedom to work in the outside world brings a certain economic pride, yet, desperate poverty forces this on the Dalit women, and, as I have been exploring, her work possibilities are restricted, and overshadowed frequently by the fear and the reality of sexual harassment.

So a very ambiguous picture emerges. Being outside the caste system means that Dalit women are not bound by the ideology of 'husband worship.'[27] The fact that traditionally 'bride wealth' is exchanged at a marriage instead of dowry, expresses the reality

27. Gabriele Dietrich, 'The Relationship between Women's Movements and Dalit Movements: Case Study and Conceptual Analysis', in Gabriele Dietrich, *A New Thing on Earth: Hopes and Fears Facing Feminist Theology* (Delhi: ISPK for TTS, Madurai, 2001), p. 204.

that Dalit women have a recognized economic value. The wedding gifts can flow in both directions, indicating a more symmetrical relationship.[28] Divorce is a far more common occurrence among Dalits than among caste Hindus, and widows are allowed remarriage. Thus there is a socially-sanctioned way of getting out of a bitterly unhappy marriage. Also, Dalit women are conscious of their relatively greater control over their lives, compared with 'upper-caste' women:

> If the water in her house runs out, she just has to sit and wait till she can find someone to go fetch the water for her. We can go and get water whenever we need it.[29]

But this is a factor easy to over-emphasize. The basic situation is that it is almost impossible for a woman to resist the social compulsion to marry, and a Dalit girl – even a child – may be forced into a marriage only to experience cruelty and violence.

Another factor is that because of the growing influence of right-wing, fundamentalist Hinduism, the situation is changing for the worse: even if the expectations of dowry were not traditionally part of the Dalit marriage customs, social mobility has meant that 'Sanskritisation' or assimilation to the customs of caste-Hindus is frequent.

Muli – whom we met above – describes his inauspicious marriage to Kia in great detail. It was inauspicious due to money problems, his own ill-health, the date chosen and the fact that the horoscopes of the couple did not match.[30] Yet the actual ceremony in his case was very similar to a high-caste ceremony. In practice there are many local variations – gifts to local goddesses, for example, animal sacrifices and celebrations on a more modest scale, indicating economic status.

What seems to be the case among many Dalit communities is that marriage is regarded as a practical contract and the expectations of happiness are not great. There is little training or education about sex for girls, so a young girl's first experiences can be both painful and miserable.

28. Jack Goody and S.J Tambiah, *Bride Wealth and Dowry* (Cambridge: Cambridge University Press, 1973), p. 347.

29. Fernando Franco, Jyotsan Macwan, Suguna Ramanathan (eds), *The Silken Swing: The Cultural Universe of Dalit Women* (Calcutta: Stree, 2000), p. 87.

30. Freeman, *Untouchable*, pp. 174–75.

> In the case of the woman ...neither marriage nor parenthood is intimately linked with sexual gratification (which is not to say that this does not occur secondarily within these institutionalised roles). In the case of the male, libidinal desire is recognised and validated, and marriage for him is recognised as a means of sexual release as much as a means by which he becomes a parent...sexed reproduction is the essential, female experience. The rituals go a long way towards constructing this ideology of motherhood.[31]

Yet Dalit women will still say that if they get love and consideration from their husbands, 'all work is bearable'.[32] Control of female sexuality and its relationship with caste purity is such an important area connected with the origins of Untouchability that it will need further attention.

Control of female sexuality is also maintained by wife-beating, and this is still common, and seems to be tolerated unless there is an active Women's Group, or local Self-Help Group to provide active resistance. I observe that in the many Self-Help Groups set up by our partners in the Thar Desert and in the Aravali Hills of Rajasthan, taking a stand against wife-beating is a high priority.

> Life is a pan on fire.
> You have to get burns first
> To get your bread later...[33]

Thus speak eight Dalit women from Delhi who tell their story in great detail.[34] They give an overall picture as to how women cope in the midst of poverty and the suffering of different kinds of sexual exploitation. Yet even if their lives are marked by this violence, they can also experience great tenderness. Whereas sexual submission may be a duty, it can also be an area of pleasure. A great problem for women, already noted above, is the extent to which men are victims to alcoholism and drugs – which of course increases women's vulnerability to violence, as will be explored in the following chapter. Married women find their day-to-day solace in the company of other women. Every Dalit colony tends to have

---

31. Franco *et al.*, *The Silken Swing*, p. 50.

32. Franco *et al.*, *The Silken Swing*, p. 92.

33. Poem by Bahinabai Chaudhari, an illiterate Marathi poetess of the nineteenth century, in Sumitra Bhave, *Pan on Fire, 8 Dalit Women Tell their Story* (New Delhi: Indian Social Institute, 1988).

34. Poem by Bahinabai Chaudhari in Bhave, *Pan on Fire*.

some form of Women's group – whether or not this functions effectively. Leela – who got good grades at school in English, but was prevented from pursuing studies through discrimination – relates:

> We have a Women's Circle here in our colony. It doesn't do a thing for anybody...But I go there with slates and pencils and teach them to read and write, teach them stories about Babasaheb (= Dr Ambedkar), teach them songs and poems.[35]

There did not seem to be any such solace for Kia, Muli's wife, only 14 years old, who remained in her deceased father's house for nine months after her marriage, while her new husband Muli travelled with the prostitute, Lakhi. Then Muli remembered he had a wife, and heard that a demon, apparently named 'Chandi', a form of the mother goddess,

> Had entered my wife's body while she was collecting dried leaves from a mango grove.[36]

He set off to find his wife and bring her to his family home. Her family had had to pay a high-caste magician to rid her body of the spirit of the goddess. Muli found her weak and feverish but recovered. The interesting feature of this story is that the demonic possession is related to the social problems and tensions experienced by Kia. Freeman explains:

> Kia was probably calling attention to her plight, as suggested by the words the spirit within her is said to have uttered. "...I came from that hill. Why aren't people worshipping me? That's why I am travelling forth without finding any shelter." Demonic possession often occurs among young Indian women confronted with personal conflicts they are afraid to discuss.[37]

Although Kia survived this particular trial and went on to bear a son in the following year, this was not the end of her marital suffering. For Muli later relates that he was tricked into marrying a second wife by her family. Kia's grief at this desertion was immense, so much so that Muli was surprised by the degree of her devotion. (Since Muli contributed almost nothing to the family income, Kia's devotion must have been genuine). Yet she had much to

---

35. Poem by Bahinabai Chaudhari in Bhave, *Pan on Fire*, p. 181.
36. Freeman, *Untouchable*, pp. 188–89.
37. Freeman, *Untouchable*, Chapter 15, pp. 188–93.

endure before he finally came to his senses and his second wife, Tafulla, returned to her family village. (Muli tried to explain his extraordinary action of taking a second wife as trickery, being put under a spell by Tafulla's family).

This story also reveals another source of solace for married women – her parents' home. Unless the parents are hostile, or desperately poor, it is accepted that she may return home for a period from time to time, perhaps for periods of between a fortnight and two months. As the writers of the study referred to above, *The Silken Swing*, relate:

> Women will leave their marital home if they feel overworked. They have an accepted practice of *risamane*, whereby a woman who is unhappy at her in-laws' home goes back to her natal home "in a sulk". We have found many cases where women use this practice to resist excessive overwork, particularly if they are living with their mother-in-law.[38]

This is an important fact: women who ran their own independent households have had different experiences from those who share the house with their husband's family and are under the authority of their mothers-in-law. Fatigue and resentment is continually expressed, mostly in relation to household chores. The women who told their stories in *Pan on Fire* were unanimous in declaring that women who suffered all their lives from domination in their parental homes, followed by being under the strict discipline of a mother-in-law, would themselves discover their own authoritarian voice and power in governing the life of their own daughter-in-law. But quarrels are not really about work-sharing:

> At issue is an attempt at self-assertion by each of the two women who have to share the domestic space and therefore compromise on their independence.[39]

In addition to visits to her parental home, a married woman may also derive great support, both emotional and financial support, from her brothers. This is something very special to Indian culture – that the tie with a brother may be stronger than with her own husband and his family. It is expected to carry on throughout a woman's life.

38. Fernando Franco, Jyotsan Macwan, Suguna Ramanathan (eds), *The Silken Swing: The Cultural Universe of Dalit Women* (Calcutta: Stree, 2000), p. 88.
39. Franco *et al.*, *The Silken Swing*, p. 92.

But perhaps the most important feature in the daily lives of Dalit married women is the way they negotiate their spaces of freedom. If we think that Dalit women are excluded from so many social areas – temple, the caste *panchayat*, Festivals, cremation grounds, the room of a newly-delivered woman – all these areas being governed by norms of ritual purity – then spaces for social interaction are crucial.[40] (Also, in the school Dalit children are frequently excluded from singing and performing in festival celebrations, activities which could give a degree of self-esteem).

The important point here is the way women negotiate these spaces in their constant see-saw-ing between power and powerlessness. What seems as a negative prohibition can actually achieve a positive end:

> The taboos on menstrual blood and foetal waste are open restrictions on women's mobility, and yet women turn them to creative use.[41]

Thus, 'her hands are not clean', meaning that she is menstruating, can provide an excuse for avoiding work that needs to be done. Even veiling the face, while appearing to be adhering to dictates of modesty, can be used as a way of maintaining privacy. Journeys to the well, for water and for washing are opportunities for companionships and support and give respite from the daily chores. In the study of the Vankars referred to, nearly 60 percent have toilets/bathrooms, yet women prefer to go out to the well or the lake for ablutions. Young girls in particular will use this as an escape route from the daily chores. Clearly, these are forms of latent protest against the oppressive nature of their lives, but, as the authors of the *Silken Swing* write:

> They have a value insofar as they make the insufferable endurable, but they "channel into subterfuge and symbolic reprisal indignation and hostility that might otherwise be directed towards modes of protest which have the potential to force fundamental transformations in the relationships between subordinate and superordinate groups".[42]

So, in conclusion to this chapter, we have seen how both the fact of journeying for fodder and water, the need to travel to the cities for

40. Franco *et al.*, *The Silken Swing*, Chapter 4, *Negotiating Spaces*, pp. 97–128.
41. Franco *et al.*, *The Silken Swing*, p. 122.
42. Franco *et al.*, *The Silken Swing*, p. 127.

work such as cleaning, sweeping or scavenging makes women constantly vulnerable to sexual harassment and exploitation and even rape – as we have seen in connection with water. She is vulnerable too in the complex relationships of the extended family – although I have tried to explore areas where Dalit women may experience greater freedom than their Rajput sisters. So sexual exploitation is one of the key defining differences between the situation of Dalit women and men. But sexual humiliation as such defines the situation of Dalit women far more than it does caste women. Dalit women grapple with brutal caste violence, caste driven gender violence, violence within their own homes and even caste enforced prostitution. Hence the next area of examination of the current scene has to be the worsening crimes of violence against Dalit women.

Chapter 3

RELIGION, VIOLENCE AND DALIT WOMEN

Even the killing of a Dalit woman is explicitly justified as a minor offence for the Brahmins: equal to the killing of an animal (Code of Manu)[1]

Uttar Pradesh Leads in Atrocities

According to recent figures tables in Parliaments by the National Commission for Scheduled Castes and Scheduled Tribes, the number of cases of atrocities against Dalits registered in 2000, stood at 23,742 cases (including 1,034 cases of rape). Dalit women are estimated to be the first victims, in close to 75 percent of these cases. The State of Uttar Pradesh leads in the number of cases registered under the Scheduled Castes/Scheduled Tribes (Prevention of Atrocities) Act 1989, followed by Rajasthan, Madhya Pradesh, Andhra Pradesh, Tamil Nadu, Karnataka, Gujarat and Bihar (Ruth Manorama, Dalit activist and award winner).

The focus of this book is to explore and highlight to what extent religion is responsible for violence against Dalit women. This is a complex reality: from the outset I have told how violence appears to be justified by the Code of Manu and re-affirmed by Hindu Scriptures. But this, itself an enormous injustice, is neither the beginning nor the end of the story. It does not explain why violence was not eliminated by the rise of consciousness of Human Rights, and the struggle against patriarchal oppression. There are complex dimensions to the story – including the way India's religions resisted caste, the relation of caste to purity and pollution, and the attitudes of two the founding fathers of the constitution, Gandhi and Dr Ambedkar. This chapter continues the narrative of the last two in uncovering the extent of violence against Dalit women. It also reveals the pseudo-religious base of one of the worst forms of violence disguised as religion – Temple prostitution – as well as the

1. Cited in Tamil Nadu Women's Forum, *Unheard Voices – Dalit Women* (Chennai, Tamil Nadu Women's Forum, 2007).

sex-worker trade. The following two chapters tackle some casual factors.

The Extent of Violence

The last two chapters have described how Dalit women are vulnerable to sexual harassment in the work situation and that their relative freedom of movement can exacerbate their vulnerability to this. The reality is that Dalit women suffer violence on a spectrum ranging from insults, accusations of low morals and loose living, sexual harassment of many sorts, to beatings and even gang rapes. In fact, when a Dalit woman is raped it is often not called 'rape' and it is not reported as such.

According to the report of the Scheduled Caste/Scheduled Tribe Commission (SC/ST) in 2002, there was an 8 percent rise in crimes against women in India, especially Dalit women. Three Dalit women are raped every day, it is reported, and are victims of caste violence. Luke Harding (*The Guardian* reporter cited in Chapter 2), says that less than 5 percent of cases make it to court.[2] Two-thirds of violent incidents are not pursued due to lack of evidence, a fact that underscores the fear of the victim and intimidation of witnesses and refusal of police to follow up the cases. One of the most important tasks of the Centre for Dalit Rights (CDR) in Jaipur, Rajasthan, is to monitor the legal process at every stage. Their documentation reports in detail the difficulties experienced in achieving for Dalits the rights that are enshrined in law.

Violence against women within marriage is condoned within the Code of Manu, cited above:

> Rape within marriage is quite common. Often men force their wives to have sex; the husband feels it's his right and duty because she is his wife. He may beat her, and she rarely says anything to anyone about it, because that would bring shame upon her. In any case there is nowhere for her to go as she has no economic independence.[3]

If women escaped to their own family home, it is probable that she would be sent back to her husband.

2. Luke Harding, 'Sex Hell of Dalit Women Exposed', *The Guardian*, New Delhi, 9 May 2001.

3. Valerie Mason-John, *Broken Voices: Untouchable Women Speak Out* (New Delhi: India Research Press, 2008), pp. 57–58.

Yet, the evidence suggests that although Dalit women do suffer violence from their own men-folk, sometimes on a daily basis, a violence that is frequently accepted, as I noted in the previous chapter – *it is upper-caste violence that is the real threat to Dalit women, especially in the rural areas.* Here we explore in more detail some of the presumed religious links, as well as other related areas of violence.

The family violence against women connected with dowry (such as dowry deaths) is more systemic with upper-caste Hindus than with Dalits (who may fight back) and backward castes unless they become prosperous and begin a process of absorbing caste marriage practices, (or Sanskritization). As Gabriele Dietrich writes:

> Against such violence, the men of the Dalit community can often not "protect their women" and it is therefore perceived as a collective weakness and vulnerability.[4]

It is also interpreted as a collective imposition of God's law: – fatalism is at work again, but, what is strange to Western consciousness, is the way that every aspect of living is governed by a legal system with a religious basis. This gives caste legitimacy and a total comprehensiveness.

Rape – A Weapon in the Caste War

Rape, as Dietrich relates, may now be considered as a weapon in the caste war. Raping Dalit women is also seen as a way of humiliating Dalit men, powerless to retaliate.[5] Rape is associated with dishonour: but Dalit women are considered to be without honour to begin with, hence rape is considered as a minor offence, as the above quotation revealed. Parading Dalit women naked around the village or town is another way of humiliating Dalit men through the suffering of their wives.

Violence may be even taken as normal and women end up doubly deserted – by the Women's Movement, who may not be operating in the countryside, and by their own Dalit men, 'who may have

4. Gabriele Dietrich, 'The Relationship Between Women's Movement and Dalit Movements: Case Study and Conceptual Analysis' in Gabriele Dietrich, *A New Thing on Earth, Hopes and Fears Facing Feminist Theology* (Delhi: ISPK for TTS, Madurai 2001), p. 204.

5. See also, John C.B. Webster, *From Role to Identity: Dalit Christian Women in Transition* (Delhi: ISPCK CTE 13, 1995), p. 17.

their own patriarchal interests in using or suppressing an assault on women'.[6]

A particularly shocking example is the caste Hindu backlash against Dalit women in Karnataka:

> In Karnataka, the atrocities that occur in the backlash against Dalit females – rape, public humiliation, and violence are used as coercive forms of domestic terrorism. For example, on September 6th 1988, in a village in Karnataka State, the powerful caste Hindus went to a Dalit household, beat up the son, looted the house, and dragged out the teenage daughter Geeta, and raped her in front of Dr Ambedkar's statue. The reason cited in the *Indian Express* was that the upper-caste Hindus do not tolerate the prosperity of Dalits.[7]

Even if this were a legitimate motive, which it certainly is not, what is the reason that the truth of the story – and similar incidents – could not be told?

These examples have to be contextualized within the fundamentalizing policies of the ruling Bharata Janata Party (BJP), and its extreme right wing, the Rashtriya Swayamsevak Sangh (RSS): the fact of the systematic Hindu-ization of all institutions in India, has an impact on the incidence of violence against Dalits, particularly Dalit women.

Experiments on the Bodies of Dalit Women

Another form of violence is the control of women's bodies by making them special targets of population control. Moses Seenarine writes of the horror stories related by Dalit women as to how they and their sisters have been butchered in 'family planning camps'

> often without their knowledge of what had been done to them. Injectable contraceptives and other hormone drugs are tested on these powerless, voiceless women by unscrupulous multi-national businesses.[8]

Pregnant women have been attacked by the police, their genitals mutilated and miscarriages caused to their foetuses when they

6. Webster, *From Role to Identity*.
7. Moses Seenarine, *Dalit Women: Victims or Beneficiaries of Affirmative Action Policies in India – A Case Study*, Brown Bag Lecture, S. Asian Institute, Columbia University, 10 April 1996, pp. 1–12.
8. Seenarine, *Dalit Women*, p. 5.

appealed to the police for help. The *Unheard Voices* Report from Tamil Nadu (2007) relates how a doctor removed a kidney from a Dalit woman (aged 45), and the police refused to register her complaint. The victim has now written to the President of India.

These stories can be multiplied many times over, and are further proof of Gabriele Dietrich's claim that violence against Dalit women is a powerful tool of the caste war. If women resist they receive further violence, as the story below shows:

> Azhagammal, a 27 year-old woman, from the district of Sivaganga, faced resistance from the panchayat (district council) in her attempts to gain a divorce from her husband two years ago.[9] She was then ordered to hand over her child to her husband. A campaign of humiliations and fines followed her refusal to do so. Eventually, when the matter was referred to the District Collector, plain clothes policemen entered her house, beat her unconscious, and then beat her outside with a log. When she regained consciousness she was in a police station – and then taken to a Government Hospital where she received only first aid. Eventually a Women's Legal Aid Centre had her admitted to the hospital for extensive treatment for multiple injuries to her thighs and back. The case was submitted as a human rights violation, following the comment that "the police need not have used force" – but what hope of justice could she ever hope to achieve?
>
> (This incident, evidence of the old Panchayat [District Council] way of handling violent incidents against Dalit women, will be seen to be one of the areas increasingly tackled by NGOs at national and international levels).

Temple Prostitution

This is an area shrouded with ambiguity and double-speak. In the first place, there is a custom, driven by extreme poverty, or the sickness of the husband, for young Dalit girls 'being married to the god':

> When I was six I was married to the god Khandoba. This is a god that many Scheduled Caste families worship in Maharashtra.[10]

9. See R. Llangovan, 'A Dalit Damned for Defying her Village,' http://hinduonnet.com/theHindu/2002/08/04

10. Valerie Mason-John, *Broken Voices: Untouchable Women Speak Out* (New Delhi: India Research Press, 2008), pp. 44–46.

This child's mother, persuaded to relinquish her daughter – for a price – did so in the belief that her husband would be cured from his illness. There was a genuine marriage ceremony:

> I had a proper marriage, with guests throwing flowers and rice at me. My name was placed on a register, and the temple people told my mother that she had to remember that I was married to Khandoba, and that I had to be completely loyal to this god for the rest of my life.[11]

Although she was taught to sing and dance for the god, and in fact lived her whole life in loyal service, her own brothers threw her out of the house, and were ashamed of her.

But, historically speaking, the most shocking area of violence against Dalit women is their being forced to become temple prostitutes or *Devadasis*. Temple prostitution differs from the many other sorts of prostitution from which women and young girls are exposed to, including trafficking in the flesh trade. Women are driven by poverty to become prostitutes or forced into the flesh trade by unscrupulous men. In our own project, we have been involved in an educational project for the children of prostitutes, *Project Asha*, managed by our partners GSMI[12] in Dudu, Jaipur. The mothers of these children are tribal people, from the Nut tribe, who have traditionally practised prostitution, and who have great difficulty in moving into another occupation, as they are landless, and have no skills, education, or trade.

Many tribes in India employ their women as prostitutes. For example, the Bancharas, Nuts, Sansis, Kanjars. Among the Bedias and the Bancharas prostitution is practised openly – by the others, covertly. The Bedias forbid marriage within the tribe and initiate their daughters into prostitution, actually celebrating their deflowering.[13] (Sad to relate, and a source of shame, from a British point of view, as we now attempt to take responsibility for past actions, these tribes once made a livelihood in the princely courts, before the British conquest, by entertaining – singing, dancing, juggling, acrobatics – or spying. With the British conquest the Rajahs lost most of their power, and this form of patronage largely ceased).

11. Mason-John, *Broken Voices*, p. 45.
12. GSMI= Gram Seva Mandal Idankabas.
13. See Debashis Mukerji, 'Brothel Buster,' *The Week*, 25 January 1998. This tells the moving story of one man, Ram Sanehi, himself of the Bedia tribe, who struggled to free the women of the tribe from prostitution.

But temple prostitution, practised by Dalits on their women and girls, is of another order, namely violence sanctioned by religion. Burnad Fatima describes this as the most serious violation of human rights and gives the example of the shoemakers, Arunthathiar, who practice *Mathamma* – or dedicating their Dalit girl children to the goddess Mathamma:

> Due to the lack of medical services, people go to Mathamma temples believing that the goddess has healing powers when the Dalit girl is sick. She is taken to the temple and left there, till her sickness is cured ... Once the child is cured, the child is named after Mathamma, and married to the goddess with the "pottu Thali" (wedlock). After she becomes a dancer and belongs to the temple. During temple festivals she dances and earns her livelihood. She is not treated with respect and publicly humiliated by men who harass her sexually... Once the girl is married to Matthamma she cannot marry others to lead a family life. Men take her as a partner, exploit her and leave her with a child.[14]

Desperate poverty is the main reason lying behind this practice as is seen by the story of Yellama, now 50 years old. She is a Dalit woman from Karnataka, from the village of Manvi where there is a Hindu temple.

> Yellama was 9 years old when her parents sold her for 4$ to an upper-caste man. He gave her a sari and a blouse, and paid for the alcohol at the initiation celebration. After that, she became his unpaid concubine begging for money and breaking stones for construction sites to support herself.[15]

Yet even now, the article reports, she refuses to remove the gold and black beaded necklace that is the symbol of her dedication, even though her blood boils at what was done to her. The necklaces symbolize the bondage that defines Devadasis girls from the lowest caste whose parents have given them to local goddesses or temples as human 'offerings.' In some villages, Devadasis are kept as concubines by the men who bought them. In others they are public chattels, who can be used by men free of charge.

> "Only in this aspect do Untouchables suddenly become touchable," says Sister Bridget Pailey, a nun who does social

14. Burnad Fathima, Speech on Dalit Women, Committee for the Elimination of Racial Discrimination, Geneva, 8–9 August 2002, p. 3.

15. Carla Power, '"Becoming a Servant of God!" Devadasis are Dalit women sold into sexual slavery', *Newsweek*, 25 June 2000.

work among Devadasis in Karnataka. "The upper-castes wouldn't drink from the same glass as a Devadasi, but they make use of her body."[16]

Such dedications of Devadasi girls have been supervised by village priests in southern India for thousands of years. Although the British tried to outlaw the tradition, and it is banned by the Indian government, according to human-rights activists, as many as 15,000 girls in rural areas are still dedicated to God each year, poverty being the driving factor. The Sisters of the Good Shepherd are one of many groups – including now efforts from the Government – who have been fighting *Devadasi* practices for 20 years, through a variety of methods, including encouraging resistance among the Devadasis themselves:

> If Devadasis get angry at their parents for selling them off, they tend not to express it openly, says Pailey. Instead, it emerges in depression or aggression, often directed against their children. Recently, a few Devadasis even spoke out against the system on All-India Radio.[17]

North Karnataka has practised temple prostitution among four Dalit sub-castes for many years. There are many justifications of the practice, ranging from the claim that if the parents are childless the child was dedicated before her birth, to the excuse that the girl has developed 'jat' or matted hair, which signifies her call to the goddess Yellama.[18] It is claimed that the system pre-dated the Aryan invasion and is associated with matriarchal traditions of the Dravidians. In any case, it seems to have an ancient origin generally in South India, providing parents of the child a ritualistic and legendary excuse to turn their girl-child into a prostitute and make a living through her. Although there is a theory that the exploitation may have occurred at a later historical stage, the first stage of the system being a dedication of the girl to the earth goddess, Yellama. With the Aryanisation of this custom the *Devadasis* were born. (I am aware that this brings us to a controversial area of the origins of Untouchability – to be argued in the next chapter). Yet, when we consider that one of the alternatives for the unwanted girl-child

16. Power, '"Becoming a Servant of God!"'
17. Power, '"Becoming a Servant of God!"'
18. The source for this section is the *Joint Women's Programme* team, 'The Devadasi System in N. Karnataka,' in BANHI 1981/2. JWP's main office is in New Delhi.

has been and still is infanticide – a fact borne out by population figures in the poorest states – then, is this a better or worse option?

Rather than an extensive study of the practice I want to discover precisely the situation now for Dalit women. One of the worst consequences today, as distinct from former times, is that becoming a *Devadasi* is very likely now to end in commercial prostitution, as many women leave – or are forced to leave – for the brothels of Mumbai (Bombay). In *Wells for India's* Project *Asha* (referred to above) the children are also vulnerable to being kidnapped and taken off to Mumbai for the same reason. *It is reported by several social studies that Dalit women form 90 percent of the sex worker trade.* Countless stories attest to the way vulnerable young girls are tempted by the offer of work, and escaping forced marriage, to leave their village for the city, where there is little chance of escape from the sex trade.

For example, the *Joint Women's Program* report that one of the main points in transit in the girl traffic pipeline is Nipani in the Begaum district. Another is Athani. Nipani has a working class population of 25,000 of whom a majority are women and large numbers are Dalits. There are 800 prostitutes of whom 200 are Devadasis. In Athani, according to one spokesman, 98 percent of families practised prostitution and had up to three girls to trade. Formerly, it is said that this practice may have been used by Dalit parents to achieve upward mobility by a liaison between their daughter and an upper-caste man. It may also have been forced on lower caste people to secure desirable and good-looking women for their pleasure. It is also possible, say the *Joint Women's Programme*, that,

> The system was designed to kill whatever vestiges of self-respect the untouchable castes have in order to subjugate them and keep them underprivileged.[19]

Now the practice has to be put in context of the economic policies and environmental crises mentioned earlier. The Devadasi belt – the strip including the border districts of Karnataka and Maharashtra – is prone to drought and has been environmentally neglected for centuries. But here grinding poverty and hunger have coincided with a vicious system by which upper-caste men get access to lower caste women with religious sanction.

19. *Joint Women's Programme* team, 'The Devadasi System in N. Karnataka,' p. 19.

For women themselves, it is possible that the sense of being devoted to the goddess, for example, Yellama, helps them to survive, since they do not endure social stigma – this may even bestow a certain prestige, as they are asked to be present at auspicious functions in the homes of the higher castes. Compared with urban prostitutes the incidence of disease is not as high in Temple prostitutes – yet the women tend to look much older than they actually are. But even if the mothers have managed to eke out some kind of dignity, their children are suffering as the social stigma attaches to them when, increasingly, more communities do not want to marry into a Devadasi family. The Bill outlawing this practice came into being in 1982 – the progress in its implementation in another story. The reasons are a complex mixture of the lack of any political will to implement the legislation in the Constitution protecting the rights of Dalits, plus the self-interest involved in keeping the system going, together with the inbuilt difficulty of succeeding in winning court cases.

A personal story strengthens this point in connection with Project *Asha*, mentioned above. In 1995, we had a small conference in the Project Headquarters in Dudu, Rajasthan. It included about 30 women, the men who controlled them and the Asha children, plus the field workers and ourselves. We were addressed by Mrs Jyotsna Chatterjee of the Joint Women's Programme, Delhi. Her words were very empowering to these women who had little hope of escaping prostitution. To us afterwards she said:

> You must keep on with what you are doing, even if it seems to have little success as regards these women. This is a deep-rooted issue and the government of India has no solution. Indeed we know there to be collusion between the police, government officials and business men.

Her words still ring in my ears.

Fear of Violence as Preventing Social Progress

Caste violence, rape and prostitution are immense problems for Dalit women and present the most prominent forms of oppression. But equally important in terms of the social progress of the young Dalit girl is the fear of violence she faces in her daily life. The low literacy rate among Dalit women has already been mentioned: it is usually ascribed to a lack of opportunity, low motivation, or that the child is a needed for child care at home – all important factors. But many sources – including Moses Seenarine who was quoted above – point to violence as a motive for parents not sending Dalit girls to school, or the girls' own unwillingness to attend. She may be afraid of physical punishment or sexual abuse at school, even perhaps from the teacher. Many incidents vouch for the reality of this fear. The journey itself, if she lives far away, may be too dangerous for her. The social stigma of being Dalit is another inhibiting factor. This is without considering other motives like education for girls being seen as a threat to Dalit patriarchy or early marriage interrupting education. However, access to education is an area currently being tackled by hundreds of social activists and NGOs – our own included. Research indicates that even in the UK bullying of Dalit children occurs in schools – usually from upper-caste children. White British children are normally unaware of caste tensions – at least at primary level.

Violence within the home in terms of domestic violence, violence outside the home in terms of sexual harassment, rape and social stigma; unjustly criticized for 'loose living' – these are the burden of Dalit women. These are all forms of violence targeting the bodies of Dalit women, already vulnerable through malnutrition, lack of access to health care and overwork. The situation is changing in certain aspects mostly because of the efforts of Dalit women themselves and growing eagerness for social change. Here I have introduced the relationship with religion in two ways. The first is the responsibility for the Code of Manu in reinforcing caste-ism – which needs to be examined more carefully. The second is the context of the rigidifying of Hinduism in the contemporary context, with a consequent backlash against those who are considered to be outside its structures. But even if Hinduism is the main religion in India, India is a secular country, yet a very religious one, and the attitudes of other faiths needs to be explored. The main causal factor to be considered, (already hinted at), far more than the collusion of religion, is that of impunity, as noted by The Hague Convention on Dalit Women's Rights in 2006:

> When considering discrimination and violence against Dalit women, one can state that impunity is *the key problem* Dalit women face today – not only while seeking legal and judicial redress for violence, but also while attempting to access and enjoy their fundamental rights and freedoms. Perpetrators enjoy virtual

immunity from prosecution for violence against Dalit women, as the police, who themselves often harbour caste prejudices, wilfully neglect to enforce the law. Not only the police, but perpetrators and their communities use their political, social and economic power to silence Dalit women, thereby denying them access to justice. The nature of collusion between state and dominant caste actors is such that the modern rule of law has no place in the hierarchical order of socioeconomic and political power relationships, as caste-based power supersedes state-derived executive authority.[20]

Before exploring further the causality of the religions my next step will be a step into the past: I will ask how the whole condition that constructed Untouchability could have occurred, especially in its implications for the social situation of Dalit women.

20. *The Hague Declaration on the Rights of Dalit Women*, The Hague, November 2006.

Chapter 4

PURITY AND POLLUTION: THEIR ROLE IN A WORSENING OPPRESSION

I am between 70 and 75 – I don't know exactly because my birth date was never recorded. I came from a village near Satara in Maharashtra, where I was treated as "Untouchable." As a young girl I had to walk with my hands behind my back, holding a broom so that when I walked my footsteps were wiped out and the Brahmins would not be polluted by them ... Whenever our shadow fell on a Brahmin, they would run with fear and sprinkle water over us, because they thought that if they stepped into our shadow they would be polluted. The only time we were allowed near the Brahmins' houses was when one of their animals died, and then we would have to drag it away – Valerie Mason-John[1]

The Indian obsession with impurity culminates in untouchability: the relegation of the Untouchables to the Bottom of the Ladder is therefore religious in nature – L. Dumont[2]

Notions of purity and pollution are so intertwined with casteism and oppression, together with their religious underpinning, that they need special focus. To do this, this chapter first focuses on the intersection of caste oppression with patriarchy and then explores the different theories as to the origins of the caste system and resulting oppression of Dalits. What role do notions of purity play in religions? Is their real focus *control* rather than any genuine religious motif? *This* is the deeper question.

The Intersection of Caste Oppression and Patriarchy

The fact that Dalit women continue to suffer such a terrible degree of discrimination and violence, as previous chapters have shown,

1. Valerie Mason-John, *Broken Voices: Untouchable Women Speak Out* (New Delhi: India Research Press, 2008), p. 17.
2. L. Dumont, *Homo hierarchicus: Essai sur Le Système des castes* (Paris: Gallimard, 1966), p. 39.

even given a certain degree of progress in education and attainment of professional positions and political representation, cries out for further investigation. Deeper factors must be at play to explain why Dalit women continue to internalize their inferiority and subjugation in what is called *subaltern consciousness*. For instance, why do notions of purity and pollution affect the lives of Dalit women far more than men's, if both are involved in what are considered humiliating occupations? It is here that we see the intersection of patriarchy and caste oppression, indicating that we cannot tackle one without factoring in the other. It is also here that religion has to be factored in, since purity and pollution have religious signification across the faiths.

It is here equally that we need to remind ourselves that even when attention was paid to the oppressed situation of Indian women by the British in the nineteenth century, it was to upper-caste women that attention was mainly directed. (To an extent this is still true today with Western interest focusing on *sati* and dowry deaths, attention that is kept alive by such popular TV series in Britain as *The Jewel in the Crown* and *The Far Pavilions:* simultaneously perception of and interest in enduring caste oppression is minimal).

Whereas it is true that Dalit women see liberation in terms of removing *caste* oppression, the heavy burden of patriarchy is inextricably bound up with the way caste is experienced. As I have said, Hindu high-caste women also experience harsh restrictions in their lives and control of their sexuality. Lack of freedom of movement, the rules of purdah, dowry deaths and domination by their husbands are all serious social issues. Although in Rajasthan the experience of *Wells for India's* partners is that drought-related poverty is a great leveller that affects Rajput women as much as tribal women in the remoter desert areas,[3] yet the maintenance of the ritual purity of high-caste women is attained at the expense of the degradation of the sexuality of her Dalit sister, a degradation in which high-caste women may collude, consciously or unconsciously.

---

3. I have explained that Rajputs, originally the warrior caste, were the rulers of Rajasthan and are still very powerful, even if the Maharajahs have lost all constitutional power.

Origins of Patriarchy and Untouchability

So I begin by asking, how did patriarchy enter Indian history and socio-cultural life? Here my purpose is not engage with a complex anthropological study, but to give an overview of the main positions, always keeping the focus as to how the rise of patriarchy affected the lives of women and how its interaction with the caste system is one of the main causes of Untouchability – but not the only one. (In the next chapter I will discuss Dalits' own myths and legends of origin).

Of course, many theories of origin abound – we might be overwhelmed with the range of explanations, from Louis Dumont's theory that Untouchability arises from the Indian obsession with purity,[4] (as the above citation indicates), to Moffatt's models of outcaste, diversity and unity, others stressing the efforts to keep a closed marriage circle (endogamy), while still others emphasize the nature of the work of former Untouchables as defining their low social position.[5] Seldom is attention given specially to women's position and the intersection of discriminations from which she suffers.

The most popular explanation of the origin of patriarchy within Hinduism is to say that through the code of Manu, written down in a long process ending around 700CE, the inferiority of women was institutionally inscribed and her life surrounded with restrictions, some of which have already been mentioned. But let us probe further and factor in the origin of Untouchability itself. There is a great dispute as to whether this arose through the Aryan Conquest of indigenous peoples – around 1500 BCE, or through the clash of Aryans with the old indigenous Dravidian culture of the south. Dr Ambedkar himself had another theory: he believed that Untouchability arose from the process of a primitive tribal society passing from nomadic life to the life of a settled village community. Gabriele Dietrich provides a useful summary of different positions.[6]

4. Dumont, *Homo hierarchicus*.

5. For a full summary of these positions, see Robert Deliège, *The Untouchables of India* (trans. Nora Scott; Oxford: Berg, 1999), Chapter 2, 'Untouchability: Theories of Caste,' pp. 27–50.

6. Gabriele Dietrich, 'The Relationship between Women's Movement and Dalit Movements,' Chapter 10, in Gabriele Dietrich, *A New Thing on Earth: Hopes and Fears Facing Feminist Theology* (Delhi: ISPK for TTS, Madurai 2001), pp. 203–27.

Her work is particularly important as gender sensitivity and her resistance to simplifying the picture are strong features in her analysis.

The first position is a classic one – that of Joanna Riddle and Rama Joshi, in *Daughters of Independence: Gender, Caste and Class in India*.[7] They argue the well-known invasion theory, namely, that there was a pre-Aryan, 'matriarchal' culture:

> that was basically egalitarian and free from caste. The matrilineal culture of the Nayars in Kerala is taken to be a remnant of this stratum as well as matriliny and matrilocality in north-eastern tribes. This culture is stated to have been destroyed by the Aryan invasions which are accountable for having established the caste system as well as control over women's sexuality. Later, Brahmin codification especially in the Smritis are said to have tightened the control.[8]

Thus they explain that the more property a woman had, the more necessary it became to control her sexuality. The Code of Manu regarded *sudras* (the fourth and lowest of the castes) and women as equally contemptible. It has never to be forgotten that holding women as contemptible is enshrined in a religious code. This view is substantially the position on the origins of Untouchability of many Dalits, including Dr James Massey, and the arguments are persuasive – the related religious issues will be discussed in a later chapter.

There is also an interesting link with the theories of goddess feminists in Europe and Asia Minor: the argument is that prior to these same Aryan invasions, there were matriarchal, egalitarian cultures, (for example in Greece, Crete and Anatolia – the former Turkey), destroyed by the invasions which gave rise to patriarchy and the destruction of matriarchy.[9] This has been questioned as unhistorical by many, a lack of evidence being one of the main problems, although some authors propose that there may have been

7. Joanna Riddle and Rama Joshi, *Daughters of Independence: Gender, Caste and Class in India* (London: Zed Books, 1986).

8. Riddle and Joshi, *Daughters of Independence*, pp. 61–65.

9. See Gerda Lerner, *The Creation of Patriarchy* (Oxford: Oxford University Press, 1986).

important matricentric[10] elements to these cultures.[11] But the Aryan invasion theory is also criticized by Dr Ambedkar himself as a racist, colonial and Western invention, thought up and promoted by Brahminical scholars. Dietrich also criticizes Liddle and Roshi's position for clubbing together *sudras,* Untouchables and Adivasis (or tribal people) under one umbrella, as well as for its lack of attention to how sub-castes actually work in reality: for example, the so-called egalitarian Nayars of Kerala did in reality practice untouchability, not only towards Untouchables, 'but also towards the Nadars whose women were forbidden to wear the upper cloth'.[12]

Dietrich is concerned to widen the discussion beyond anti-Brahminical propaganda and the sexual control of women – (because this leads to an idealization of the position of Dalit women as possessing sexual freedom). She cites approvingly the views of activist Ruth Manorama (referred to earlier): Ruth Manorama is a key role model for Dalit women. She founded Women's Voice and registered the Bangalore Gruhakarmikara Sangha (Domestic Workers' union) as a trade union. At an early stage, she had realized that large, mass-based organizations were necessary to take up issues related to societal structures affecting large populations over a wide area: thus was born the National Federation of Dalit Women.[13] In 2005, Ruth Manorama was nominated for the Nobel

10. Matriarchy is the rule of society by women who would control among other things, land ownership. *Matrilineal* means that the land inheritance goes through the line of mothers, who may not be in overall control, in fact matrilineality can coexist with patriarchy. *Matricentric* means that the society is focused on the culture created by women and others – though again they are not in overall control.

11. For example, Rosemary Radford Ruether, *Gaia and God* (New York: HarperCollins, 1992).

12. Dietrich, 'The Relationship between Women's Movement and Dalit Movements,' p. 215 citing Robert Hardgrave, *The Nadars of Tamil Nadu: The Political Culture of a Community in Change* (Berkeley, CA: University of California Press, 1969), pp. 56–66.

13. Ruth Manorama was also closely associated with the mobilization of Dalits towards the World Conference Against Racism in Durban, an effort that put the issue on the international map, as we have noted. In 1993, she organized the public hearing on Violence Against Dalit Women in Bangalore, and the National Federation of Dalit Women was born out of that effort. Ruth Manorama was also a core group member of the Asian Women's Human Rights Council.

Peace prize, and in 2006 she was awarded the Right Livelihood
Award.

Ruth Manorama's focus is on how *Jati* and sub-caste actually
function and she highlights the way this triple oppression of class,
patriarchy and caste actually operates in women's lives. Yet she
concurs more or less with the Aryan invasion theory, as does a
third position, which also discusses other possible origins. This is
the position of Kalpana Kannabiran, who argues that although
the feminine power principle – *shakti* – is built into Hindu religion,
yet the worship of the goddess in no way contradicts the
institutionalized oppression of women. This is an important point:
many Christian feminists, using the example of the India pantheon
of goddesses, point out that it is simplistic to assume that a female
deity, as opposed to the 'male deity' of Christianity is going to
solve the problem of the oppression of women. A more complex
analysis is necessary.

Kannabiran understands that the subjugation of women into
slavery is very ancient, and can be traced back to the Rigvedic
hymns, even pre-Vedic, and concludes:

> It is my thesis that patriarchy is in fact the basis of the caste
> system and that the patterns of hierarchy, power and authority
> which characterise the caste system are derived from earlier forms
> of gender – based oppression.[14]

Simply to argue for a feminist based interpretation of Hinduism on
account of goddess worship is fallacious, she argues, since this can
accompany tighter caste restrictions on the lives of women. But the
drawback of this monocausal explanation, as Dietrich points out, is
that if patriarchy – which is global in its permeation – has caused
the caste system, why only in India and not elsewhere? I find this a
very persuasive argument.

Dietrich then seeks explanations that are not based on the invasion
theory: she finds these in a combination of the idea of Morton Klass
and those of Dr Ambedkar. Morton Klass, rejecting both the racial
and invasion theories, sees caste,

> mainly as marriage circle which regulates the access to resources
> in the villages and the exchange of services. The crucial step in

14. Cited in Dietrich, 'The Relationship between Women's Movement and
Dalit Movements,' p. 217.

the creation of caste in his view is therefore that from tribal exogamy to caste endogamy.[15]

Caste as controlling the marriage circle is also stressed by Dr Ambedkar, as we shall see. The strength of Morton Klass's explanation is to allow a multi-causal explanation of caste and this must be the right way forward, without necessarily ruling out the invasion and conquest theory. We will need to return to this multi-causal explanation.

The fifth type of explanation needing attention is that of the Dravidian movement of southern India which reverses the Aryan myth: on the one hand it maintains a theory of invasion seen as the cause of the caste system: on the other hand it argues for an independently ruled 'Dravida Nadu' up to the time of the British conquest. The contestable point is that Dalit leaders blame caste on the Aryan invasion and at the same time claim that an egalitarian culture was continuous in their own tradition. But the fact of the continuous oppression of women does not bear this out in reality.

The Ideas of Dr Ambedkar

The final position discussed by Gabriele Dietrich is that of Dr Ambedkar. I was very aware and impressed as to the importance of Ambedkar in the offices of one of *Wells for India's* partner organizations in the tribal areas of the Aravali Mountains south of the city of Udaipur. His portrait – wearing Western clothes, as contrasted with Gandhi's traditional homespun cotton – took pride of place. Dr Babasaheb Ambedkar – sometimes he is simply known affectionately as 'Babasaheb' – is of crucial importance to the Dalit struggle, in his function as role model, in the context of the political representation of Dalits in the Indian Constitution, in his struggle with Gandhi especially in the 'fast unto death'(1932) of the latter,[16] and final conversion to Buddhism only a few months before he died: at this point of the discussion it is his attitude to women and understanding of the origins of Untouchability that are the focus.

15. Klass, *The Emergence of the South Asian Social System*; Dietrich, 'The Relationship between Women's Movement and Dalit Movements,' p. 218.

16. Through this 'fast unto death,' an action which some would see as emotional blackmail, Gandhi 'forced' Ambedkar to give up his battle for separate representation for Dalits in the new Indian Constitution.

Bimrao Ramji Ambedkar (1891–1956), a Mahar, (a Dalit caste) was born in the village of Mahu, in Maharashtra.[17] His amazing intellectual achievements – with two doctorates, one in the USA and one in England – were partly enabled by the financial patronage of the Maharajah of Baroda. In fact, his father's job in the army of Baroda had strengthened his determination to ensure that his son was properly educated, a goal for which he made tremendous sacrifices. Eventually Ambedkar had a brilliant career as a barrister, as well as a political career that would be crucial for the political role of Dalits in the constitution.[18]

As might be expected, Ambedkar's focus was much more on the origins of caste and untouchability than on patriarchy and its effect on women. (He was married twice: whereas his first wife seemed to have remained in the background and then died, his second wife Savitabai, was of Brahmin origin, and followed him into Buddhism a few months before he died). Such general observations as the following are typical of Ambedkar:

> From time immemorial man as compared with women has had the upper hand. He is a dominant figure in every group and of the two sexes has greater prestige. With this traditional superiority of man over woman his wishes have always been consulted. Woman, on the other hand, has been an easy prey to all kinds of injunctions (religious, social and economic). But man, as maker of injunctions is most often above them all.[19]

As I have said, he rejected the invasion theory as a monocausal explanation and, like Morton Klass, saw the prohibition of intermarriage (i.e. endogamy) as the *essence* of caste. He saw the Brahmins neither as creators of the caste system, nor as having the power to impose it.[20] Rather, it spread through manipulation and imitation. Caste is not a direct continuation of *Varna*[21] but became a process in its own right, consisting of numerous splittings into

17. See Eleanor Zelliot, 'Dr Ambedkar and the Mahar Movement' Doctoral Dissertation, University of Pennsylvania, 1969.

18. For a fuller account of Ambedkar's significance, see Robert Deliège, *The Untouchables of India*, Chapter 8, pp. 175–91.

19. B.R. Ambedkar, 'Castes in India', in *Writings and Speeches, Vol.* 1 (Bombay: Government of Maharashtra, 1989), p. 11.

20. Dietrich, 'The Relationship between Women's Movement and Dalit Movements,' p. 221.

21. Varna is the fourfold division of Indian society – Brahmin, Kshatriya, Vaishya and Sudra.

endogamous units. So he rejected both the division of labour and 'purity of blood' arguments as causal explanations, since the system originated *after* populations had already become mixed, thus *after* the rules of purity and pollution. *This is crucial for the position of women.* His position is borne out by Dipankar Gupta, who challenges the traditional theory, and also insists that the notion of untouchability did not arise until at least the second century CE.[22] He also argues that caste is far more complex and should not be reduced to the Varna system. To complicate matters further, many low castes claim Brahminic origin. The Bhangi – discussed in Chapter 2 as part of the Manual Scavenging humiliation – partake of the myth that they claim descent from Brahminic origin.[23]

Ambedkar insisted that there was no racial difference between Hindus and Untouchables. (His political struggles are based on this – that there is no solid ground for discrimination in law if the racial basis is identical. It is possible to understand his conversion to Buddhism in the light of his failure to win this point).[24] His account of Untouchability is based on the distinction between Tribesmen and *Broken men* from alien tribes. So, who are these Broken Men?

Ambedkar thought that to protect the village from outside attack, guards and watchmen were hired: these were 'broken men' who had strayed from the tribe and lived as individuals. They would be given food and protection in return for their services. This makes good sense, and would also explain why Dalits live in separate colonies, some distance from the village. *Untouchability* resulted as a result of the contempt of the Brahmins of 'The Broken Men' – in the same way that there was contempt for Buddhists. The second reason is the continuation of beef-eating after it has been given up by the Brahmins. These reasons, as has been said, do not rule out the invasion theory and the fact that there were indigenous cultures which must have been displaced at this point. Tribals (Adivasis)

22. See Dipankar Gupta, *Interrogating Caste: Understanding Hierarchy and Difference in Indian Society* (New Delhi: Penguin India, 2000).

23. Gupta, *Interrogating Caste*, p. 75.

24. For example, his book, *The Untouchables: Who Were They? And Why They Became Untouchables* (New Delhi: Amrit Books, 1948), 'looks much like a myth, for it was meant to legitimate Ambedkar's attraction to Buddhism: in it he defended the idea that Brahmins hated Untouchables and held them in contempt because they were Buddhists.' Robert Deliège, *The Untouchables of India*, pp. 185–86.

claim continuity with these people and were displaced to the
mountains. It would mean that the origins of Untouchability could
be associated with movements such as anti-Buddhism and Jainism
– all these factors pointing to multi-causal explanations. In discussing
Ambedkar's views on the origins of Untouchability I have
deliberately avoided the constitutional clashes between himself and
Gandhi before Independence – to which I shall return.

But all these reasons, pollution, ritual impurity, beef-eating,
contempt for certain sorts of work, all now do not stand up as
justifications for the present stigma of Untouchability – if they ever
should have done. (For example, the story is told of a certain
sociologist Harper, walking with a Brahmin who claimed that the
Dalits [Holerus] of a certain area were beef-eaters, and hence
discriminated against. Harper knew they were not, whereupon the
Brahmin asked a man working in the field. The man replied that
they had given up more than 30 years ago. 'There you are, I told
you they ate beef,' cried the Brahmin triumphantly).[25] Such
explanations can never be adequate excuse for the de-humanizing
and degraded status of Dalits. Nor do they factor patriarchy into
the equation.

Purity and Women

So, in this study to how caste oppression affects women, the issue
of purity needs specific attention, especially as to the interactions
between patriarchy and the caste system. The restrictions on the
movement of high-caste women, the prohibition of widow remarriage, the insistence on marriage within the caste and *jat*, the
prohibition on interdining are based on notions of exclusion,
hierarchy and caste purity. Yet, as Dietrich says, quoting Ambedkar,
it is a mistake to identify Untouchables with the *Impure* as do the
Brahmins. The notion of the Impure came into existence at the time
of the Dharma Sutras (teachings on the Vedic Scriptures) whereas
the notion of Untouchability came into being much later than 400
CE.[26] Second, that the Dalit woman is seen as a threat to strict notions
of purity is to some degree a fiction, as the exploitative use made of
her body by high-caste men renders the notion of Untouchability

25. Cited by Delïege, *The Untouchables of India*, p. 50.
26. Dietrich, 'The Relationship between Women's Movement and Dalit
Movements,' pp. 222–23.

as a complete smoke-screen! Third, as Deliège points out, ritual pollution does not explain everything:

> When their work requires it, Untouchables may use village streets normally closed to them. Good also notes that, while people say that physical contact with an Untouchable is polluting, he never met anyone who actually purified himself after such a contact, and accidental contact is not taken seriously.[27]

He points out that Dalits can be medical doctors, vegetarians and scrupulously clean in personal hygiene, yet still be considered as polluted as a night soil remover (scavenger). Occupation has nothing to do with it: more germane to my argument is his statement that what it is actually about is 'cumulative domination'.[28]

The purity issue as I see it affecting women is the way caste intersects with patriarchy's control and exploitation of the bodies of women. High-caste Hindu women are kept ritually 'pure' – whereas, for example, Thakurs have the right to sleep with Chamar women and many landlords claim the 'first-night privilege' of sleeping with a just-married Dalit bride. Perhaps the notion of scapegoat is relevant here, but this vulnerability of Dalit women gives the lie to the truth of their so-called freedom. Whereas they are freer, to some extent, of the restrictions of caste patriarchy, in the sense of being able to move around more freely – linked of course with economic necessity; on the one hand they gain a grudging respect from the family for being a wage earner, but on the other they are accused of being 'loose women' with no morals and are prey, as noted, to severe sexual harassment and exploitation. It becomes very easy for them to be labelled as prostitutes. But Deliège's term of 'cumulative domination' is a useful tool to connect the commonality of oppression of Dalit women with all women.

Historically and culturally women's bodies have been ritually restricted and controlled in all religions. Their sexuality has been regarded in a derogatory manner. For example, in the Hebrew Bible, the Book of Leviticus details the restrictions around sexual intercourse and female menstruation in a way demeaning to

---

27. Deliège, *The Untouchables of India*, p. 49, citing A. Good, *The Female Bridegroom: A Comparative Study of Life – Crisis Rituals in South India and Sri Lanka* (Oxford: Clarendon Press, 1990), pp. 14–15.
28. Deliège, *The Untouchables of India*, p. 50.

women.[29] Jewish feminist, Judith Plaskow, in her ground-breaking book, *Standing Again at Sinai*, points out that Jahweh ordered the people to prepare to receive the Covenant at Sinai by taking a ritual bath and 'Do not go near a woman'.[30] In one fell swoop this clarifies that women were excluded from the founding covenant of Israel, and that it was sexual intercourse that defined this unworthiness. Her book is an alternative attempt at re-visioning the founding covenant. Again, in the Book of Exodus, Moses was criticized for marrying Zipporah, 'the Cushite woman,' clearly a darker-skinned Ethiopian. The Indian theologian, Mukti Barton, points out that feminist Christian biblical exegesis tends to focus on Miriam, Moses' sister, ignoring the suggestion that what was going on may have been the racist rejection of Zipporah – similar to the rejection of the Dalit women by caste Hindus today.[31]

The Christian Church's record on valuing and honouring women's sexuality is a scandalous history of devaluing and controlling: Mary of Magdala has – until recent feminist scholarship – been regarded as a prostitute, – and it is partly due to her very freedom in following Jesus that she is suspected, as have been many faithful Christian women.[32] Catherine of Siena was 'a woman too much on the road' and Mary Ward and her sisters in the sixteenth century, who represent the first example of active, non-enclosed women's congregations, were perceived by the religious authorities as a threat and locked up in a convent by the Poor Clares. Many patristic sources speak in disgusted tones of women's sexuality, in their efforts to glorify ascetic virginity, seeing both this and masculinity as the norm for holiness.[33] A poignant example of the way religious symbols are used to control the lives of women is the Roman Catholic nineteenth century devotion to the Virgin Mary as both Virgin and Mother – a Virgin, *Virgo Intacta*, before and after the birth of Jesus.

29. Leviticus 18–20. The many prohibitions can be understood on the basis of regulating sexual conduct: yet within this context women are the property of men.

30. Judith Plaskow, *Standing Again at Sinai: A Jewish Feminist Theology* (San Francisco, CA: Harper and Row, 1990), p. 25, citing Exodus 19.

31. See Mukti Barton, 'The Challenge of the Darker Sister' in *Feminist Theology* 27 (May 2001), pp. 61–81.

32. See Susan Haskins, *Mary Magdalen* (London: HarperCollins, 1993).

33. These are well-known and do not need repeating here. See for example, Rosemary Ruether, *Sexism and God-Talk* (London: SCM Press, 1983).

She has been held up before ordinary women as a role model of purity ('O purest of creatures', is a well-known hymn we sing) and a difficult one to follow since the message is that she remained above and untouched by sexual intercourse. And yet, at the same time in England, respectable Victorian gentlemen, in an appalling example of double standards, were making use of prostitutes, while idealizing the purity and innocence of their own wives.

Such examples throughout the history of culture and religion are easy to discover and understand within overall patterns of patriarchal control and discrimination against women.[34] They also illustrate the way the ideal of *purity* can be presented as a religious notion and held in place by religious symbols and sanctions. Further, women have been targeted as bearers of the purity of the community as a whole, and in the case of the caste system, the purity of the endogamous group.

On the face of it, the transgression of the norms of purity many seem to explain or give a rationalization for discrimination and brutal treatment against Dalit women, and certainly serves to hold in place the *subaltern* consciousness referred to. But the interpretation of the current experience of violence has more to do with the 'accumulation of levels of domination.' This is much more concerned with abuse of power, and this is not primarily about sexuality. Thus Marie Fortune, Director of the Centre for Domestic Violence, Seattle, in her pioneering book *Sexual Violence; the Unmentionable Sin*, made it very clear that sexual violence and rape were not about sex but about power. As Gabriel Dietrich said (cited earlier), 'rape is a weapon in the caste war.' Upper-caste men now increasingly humiliate Dalit men by brutally gang-raping their wives, often with the collusion of the police force. This explains why not only is a multi-strategic response needed, but that changing destructive patriarchal attitudes towards female sexuality will be ineffective without confronting the Human Rights issues of the Dalit people as a whole, on a national and international basis. *The need to confront the Churches is urgent.* It also means that the Women's Movement as a whole has to tackle caste racism as part of its structured campaign for justice for women.

34. As Mary Daly has done in *Gyn/Ecology: The Metaethics of Radical Feminism* (Boston, MA: Beacon Press, 1978).

This Chapter has tried to discover the links between the origins of patriarchy and untouchability. We have seen how patriarchal controls operate through religious restrictions and symbols, especially through the oppositions of purity and pollution. But what we have not yet seen is how religion operates in the lives of Dalit women themselves. Does religion give a strength that sustains women amidst the daily struggle? And what religion has the resources to offer this? Or is it one more burden adding to an already burdensome existence? To these questions we now turn.

Chapter 5

The Spirituality of Dalit Women – Sustaining or Oppressing?

Let me not be sad because I was born a woman in this world;
many saints suffer in this way.

Cast off all shame
And sell yourself
In the market-place.
Then alone
Can you hope
To reach the Lord – Janabai, 1298–1350ce.[1]

'The battle is in the fullest sense of spiritual'. It is a battle for
freedom; it is the battle for the reclamation of human personality
– Dr Ambedkar

Introduction

This chapter seeks to understand the religion and spirituality of
Dalit Women on their own terms. Is religion experienced as one
more burden in a woman's life or are there liberating aspects that
may ease this burden? Furthermore, is it possible to discover aspects
of Dalit women's spirituality that are transformative of the
oppressive realities that have been described in this book – or at
least aspects that offer hope of this? Spirituality is understood here
as the spiritual dimension that undergirds a person's life, expressed
in a myriad of different ways, giving meaning and coherence to
even the most trivial of everyday actions, as well as inspiring the
most idealistic expressions of human beliefs and aspirations.
Spirituality is the living out of our most cherished values. At its
best it can provide sustaining resources in the depths of suffering:

1. Janabai was born into a low-caste sudra family. She was one of the best
known and loved of Maharashtra Varkari saint poets. See Susie Tharu and
K. Lalita (eds), *Women Writing in India, Vol. 1* (New Delhi: Oxford University
Press, 1991), pp. 82–83.

at its worst, it can serve to undergird an oppressive system. Both extremes can be present in the same religion. But India is a land of many religions and the relationship of Dalits – especially women – to these are complex and in some cases ambiguous.

As is very clear, Dalit women cross the spread of all Indian religions, so the temptation to generalize must be resisted. Dalit women are also close to many ancient indigenous traditions, especially to a wealth of local goddess traditions. Conversion to Christianity and to neo-Buddhism occurred as much with Dalit women as with their men-folk. Dalit women were members of many movements for social reform such as Arya Samaj and Ad Dharm (founded by Mango Ram in the early part of the twentieth century in the Punjab, and revived later by co-opting the figure of the sixteenth century saint Ravi Dass).[2]

But did these reform movements bring the hoped for social change? And how was women's position different from men's? This chapter will be mostly descriptive in approach and the next two chapters aim to be more constructive in suggesting ways forward based on a Christian Liberation Theology perspective.

First, it needs to be explained in what sense the word 'religion' is being used, since the concept covers a diversity of customs, codes of social obligations and spiritual behaviour. Mark Juergensmeyer offers a helpful threefold distinction:[3] religion can be seen as

> *Qaum*, a large religious community such as that of the Muslims. It could also mean *panth*, the fellowship of those who revere a lineage of spiritual authority. Or again it could mean *dharm*, customs and codes of social behaviour such as those entailed by caste or ritual and implied in observing the polarity between pure and impure.

These three types may often occur in mixed forms and have undergone considerable changes through the centuries. The fellowship of *panth* was experienced in the very early Bhakti or devotional movements of the twelfth and thirteenth centuries – and we shall see that this influence continues to be very meaningful for women. Juergensmeyer points out that when lower caste people say they are not Hindu,

2. See Mark Juergensmeyer, *Religion as Social Vision: The Movement against Untouchability in 20th Century Punjab* (Berkeley, CA: University of California Press, 1982).

3. Juergensmeyer, *Religion as Social Vision*, pp. 2–3.

> They mean they are offended by the role which they are placed
> in the *dharmik* world view of the Hindus.[4]

Moreover, he maintains that,

> Untouchables seldom describe themselves as Hindu, Muslim or
> Sikh, except when political or social reasons make it expeditious
> to do so.[5]

So, only in a very broad sense could former Untouchables be called
'Hindus' and the *dharmik* sense has been explicitly rejected by many,
possibly even for centuries.

In this work, since the special focus is Dalit women, within the
general religious background I explore what values are particularly
important for women, trying always to open up areas leading to
social change. While on the one hand there will be no tightly
organized religious systematic system to be recovered (as is often
demanded by the West) on the other hand, *unlike* the West, there is
no strict sacred/profane splitting of reality. The entire world of
Dalit women is experienced as sacred. Nor can there be any one
overarching characterization of the religion of the Dalit people. And
in addition, we will discover that Dalit women are ingenious in
integrating and weaving many elements from disparate religious
sources into the fabric of their lives. A world is created where the
great deities function less powerfully than local gods and goddesses
in the lives of Dalit women.

An Earth-Related Spirituality

Traditionally, the lives of Dalit people have been lived close to the
earth, as the struggle for water and land has shown. I also pointed
out that this would have both negative and positive aspects for
women: the daily struggle for access to water still carries on, and
in 2002, all states of India were officially declared to be drought-
affected, a drought that lasted for five years in states like Rajasthan.
Yet there was no official study describing how this affected the
lives of Dalit women specifically.

The famous story of the Chipko Movement illustrates the
importance of trees for tribal women (Adivasis), and the fact that
their existence makes the difference between life and death for rural

---

4. Juergensmeyer, *Religion as Social Vision*, p. 3.
5. Juergensmeyer, *Religion as Social Vision*, p. 92.

communities.[6] Among trees held in special regard are the *pipal* and
the *banyan*. Thus the massive deforestation since Independence (1947)
directly affects the lives of tribal women, struggling to find fodder
for their animals. This heroic devotion to trees is rooted in the
example and principles of the sixteenth century founder of the
Bishnoi religion, Guru Jambeshvar. It was he who instituted the
religious practice of not cutting down green trees, a practice now
beginning to take on globally.[7] It is also suggested that for the
Bishnoi, tree protection is a symbol of resistance to the ruling Rajputs;
but this could also point:

> to the local nobility's recent attempt to co-opt an identification
> with nature and establish themselves as allied with Bishnoi
> environmental values, which are globally admired.[8]

The glorification of the memory of Amrita Devi and her companions
through tree-hugging, as this is manifested in the West, can
sometimes idealize the caste struggle, masking the fact that this
event was actually a brutal murder of Dalit (Adivasi) women. These
two points, women's courage, wisdom and respect for trees, plus
the brutality of their killing, is reflected by the following poem of
Aruna Gnanadason, Indian Ecofeminist theologian, now in Geneva:
the poem begins with the violence inflicted on the trees:

> She bleeds,
> With every lash on her body
> She weeps!
> The electric saw cuts deep...cuts quickly
> Into the gentle flesh of the trees.
> The trees weep!
> And slowly, the forests die...
> The soil dies...
> The earth dies
> And God knows that the earth weeps
> And weeps with her.[9]

---

6. This was referred to in Chapter 2.

7. See Anne Grodzins Gold and Bhoju Ram Gujar, *In the Time of Trees and
Sorrows: Nature, Power and Memory in Rajasthan* (New Delhi: 2002), pp. 248–49.

8. Grodzins Gold and Gujar, *In the Time of Trees and Sorrows*, citing R.J.
Fisher, *If the Rain Doesn't Come: An Anthropological Study of Drought and Human
Ecology in Western Rajasthan* (Delhi: Manohar, 1997).

9. Aruna Gnanadason, 'They Heal their Bodies...they Heal the Earth', *In
God's Image*, Vol. 19.2 (September 2000), p. 47.

The poem continues with the death of the women, thus evoking the connections between women, trees, earth:

> She bleeds,
> With very battering of her body
> She weeps!
> His hand has power...it cuts deeply
> Into the gentle flesh of her soul ...[10]

Then the poem begins to be a song of resistance that transforms violence into a healing earth spirituality. It ends on a note of hope and triumph linking past and present:

> Women of the Chipko Movement,
> Women of the earth,
> Women of life...
> Women survivors of violence,
> Women of hope...
> They weep no more,
> They heal their bodies,
> They heal the earth....
> And God laughs with uninhibited joy![11]

So, not only *Bishnoi* women, but countless Dalit women honour the earth and a diversity of earth goddesses as mother: energy, *(shakti)* nourishment and life are drawn from her, although this relationship has been lost to an extent through Dalits being driven from the land and forced into the oppression of bonded labour. (The present reality of struggling to find twigs and branches for firewood and fodder is well described by Anne Grodzins Gold and Bhoju Ram Gujar in their book *In Time of Trees and Sorrow*).[12]

In spite this level of suffering and women's labour of finding water, firewood and food, a love of the land, trees, plants and creatures still characterizes the spirituality of Dalit women. Rocks, stones and natural outcroppings have special significance for Dalits and are 'sometimes decorated and worshipped much like the deities in Hindu temples'.[13] This emerges in countless songs and stories. What is amazing is that even among the Bhangi people, who, as I have explained, still suffer a level of extreme discrimination as scavengers, a love of nature is still a characteristic feature. This was

10. Gnanadason, 'They Heal their Bodies...'.
11. Gnanadason, 'They Heal their Bodies...'.
12. Gnanadason, 'They Heal their Bodies...'.
13. Juergensmeyer, *Religion as Social Vision*, p. 94.

discovered by the researchers of *The Silken Swing,* a study of Dalit women in Gujurat, (cited earlier), who suggest it may have something to do with the fact that the work of the Bhangi people of tending animals, sweeping leaves, collecting cow dung and so on, keeps them out in the open air, appreciative of the environment and its vital importance. They cite a touching poem:

> O dove, go to my beloved's country;
> There are coconut trees in my beloved's country;
> O dove, go to my beloved's country.[14]

Another song invites a black cuckoo to 'our country'. The cuckoo cannot identify the place, so the song goes:

> In our country there are little streams,
> O cuckoo, come to our country.[15]

I myself have seen tribal shrines in the Aravali Hills, Rajasthan where this sense of closeness to nature prevails (See photograph below).

Tribal Shrine in Aravali Hills, Rajasthan: the priest protects his people from the snake (photograph courtesy of Mary Grey).

14. Fernando Franco, Jyotsna Macwan, Suguna Ramanathan (eds), *The Silken Swing: The Cultural Universe of Dalit Women* (Calcutta: Stree, 2000), p. 213.
15. Franco *et al., The Silken Swing.*

In the photo the priest with the sword is not killing the snake, but protecting people from its snake bite.

The sense of connectedness with nature, of loyalty to place, a tenderness in relating to birds and trees, in a context of human loving relationship, brings a whole new dimension to the lives of Dalit women – (and the songs cited are all women's songs) – whose lives we have seen are otherwise full of humiliations. It is reminiscent of the biblical *Song of Songs*, one of the few biblical expressions of lyrical human sexual love in the context of nature. Nor are these necessarily ancient songs of the past. Some recall ancient times, but others adapt to the present and new experiences. Here is a delightful song about eating ice-cream, not from a specifically religious context:

> Let us go down to the sea-shore for ice-cream!
> Whom shall we take to wash dishes?
> We'll take Anilkumar to wash dishes!
> Whom shall we take to lick leftovers?
> Ashok brother-in-law will eat left-overs!
> Who will go with us to eat ice-cream?....
> We'll take Hansa, Bharati, Darshana with us.
> Let's go to the sea-shore for ice-cream![16]

Quite apart from the glee and humour expressed in this spontaneous outing to the sea-shore, the suggestion that gender roles can be subverted – that nothing is divinely ordained, if men-folk can be ordered to wash dishes and eat left-overs is very striking. In fact, we shall see that song is a vital means of subversion and thus ripe in potential for social change for women. *It is also a valuable source for understanding women who in many cultures are the bearers of oral traditions in song and story.*

Thus, if Dalit women's spirituality could be described as cosmic, involving a respect for and identification with nature, it follows also that it is not an attempt to transcend nature in terms of otherworldly existence.[17] So an otherworldly God, Heaven and Hell find little place – in fact, goddesses dominate a this-worldly life, although Dalits are quite capable of appropriating and changing the dominant religion for their own struggle. This runs counter to the belief in traditional Hinduism, where:

16. Franco *et al.*, *The Silken Swing*, p. 203.
17. Here I am grateful for the unpublished paper of Sister Shalini, 'Dalit Women in India Today,' New Delhi, January 2003.

Karmic merit accrued during this life is directed towards a future and distant goal, the release of the soul *(moksha)* after many cycles of rebirths. For lower castes the possibility of salvation – or rather of divine protection is much more immediate, and the idea of karma is irrelevant.[18]

This must actually be a major difference from Hinduism and even Buddhism. Also, the ancient, earth-related goddesses survive and may be worshipped alongside the rituals of Hinduism, Islam, Christianity and even neo-Buddhism. John Webster writes that:

Dalits worship a whole complex of village deities in order to be saved not from anger, high excitability or even insanity, but from disease, barrenness, and other externally induced misfortunes.[19]

Transcendence, then, is not bound up with escape from karmic rebirth: it is much more a question of daily experience, of struggle and protest against the indignities of this life. So religion, far from being an opiate, is rather a means of finding strength to survive, protest and achieve some dignity in life – even if, tragically, in Christian churches the opposite has been experienced. So, whereas caste-Hindus will avoid anything that pollutes and consciously seek purifying actions because of their direct karmic consequences, these are comparatively unimportant for lower castes. Here, although the sources are clear that Dalits do not consider themselves polluting – this is an oppressive label projected on them by the caste system – yet it must be asked whether women have internalized a sense of shame, since they experience a double humiliation, also because of attitudes to female sexuality. This will be explored in the next chapter.

Given the level of humiliation heaped on women, it is not surprising that dignity is a deep-seated yearning, especially of women. This is a recent story of poor tribal women in Uttar Pradesh, when asked what they longed for by a visiting social worker:

The women were silent for some time. Suddenly, one landless woman answered:
"I want to live in dignity, I do not want to be reduced to a state of helplessness where there is no respect for me as a human being – yes, that's what I want, I want to live in dignity."[20]

18. Juergensmeyer, *Religion as Social Vision*, p. 97.
19. John Webster, *The Dalit Christians: A History* (New Delhi: ISPCK, 2000), p. 157.
20. V. Ramachandran, 'Needed: A Life of Dignity,' *The Hindustan Times*, 7 October 1999.

It was not the physical things they longed for – although they lacked almost everything – but respect and dignity. This story takes us close to the heart of the longings of Dalit women.

Dalit Women – Relationship with Goddesses

The way in which Dalit women relate to the godhead also constitutes a counter discourse for they invest the relationship with more familiarity and identification than usual in mainstream art.[21]

Throughout all religions, women's capacity for religious devotion and commitment to rituals, especially prayer and fasting, is remarkable. Dalit women are no exception. The story I begin to uncover here is both one of domesticated traditional ritual that brings consolation to daily life, together with elements of resistance to oppressive hierarchies – both within and without of Dalit circles – and of subversion of the status quo, even if only subtly expressed in story and song. The line between yearning, dreaming and the possible is crossed and recrossed in song and story – even the Bhangi people dream of conquest in their songs.

For Dalit people as a whole, goddesses are important. Sathianathan Clarke describes Paraiyar religion as revolving around a class of goddesses:

At a conceptual level, the Paraiayar believe in one, supreme, omnipresent Spiritual Being, (that which is He/She who is), or Sakti, (Divine power)…In practice, however, they tend to worship female manifestations of this supreme being.[22]

In Malaipallaiam the main goddess is Ellaiyamman, he tells us, while in Thottanavoor the main goddess venerated is Mariyamman. We will return to these important figures: the task here is to try to understand the specific impact of goddess worship on women.

With this is mind, the songs devoted to the Mother Goddess, say the authors of *The Silken Swing*, can be seen as a celebration of female power.[23] Whereas in pre-Sanskritic cultures the Mother Goddess (Mata) was always without a consort, now she has been

---

21. Franco *et al.*, *The Silken Swing*, p. 204.

22. Sathianathan Clarke, *Dalits and Christianity: Subaltern Religion and Liberation Theology in India*, (Delhi: Oxford University Press, 1998), p. 71.

23. Franco *et al.*, *The Silken Swing*, pp. 204–12.

fitted into the Hindu pantheon through Parvati, the consort of Shiva. Here the focus is on the Mother as she is worshipped and appears in the song and dance (garbha) of Dalit women:

> The *garbha* celebrated their own reproductive capacity and the link between a joyous sexuality and their capacity to procreate, customarily de-linked by mainstream patriarchal culture, is openly, gladly and rhythmically proclaimed over and over again.[24]

In these songs the Mother Goddess is given familiar human attributes. She behaves as the women do – except that she is completely free. It appears that these performances are a mixture of how things are and how they might be:

> In the process of creating divinity in their own image, they celebrate and participate in their own power.[25]

Though these are all performed within patriarchal parameters, the fact that they touch on self-esteem and riches, both attributes of power, points to the opposite of passivity and acceptance of patriarchal norms. Quite a different picture is given from the obedient, self-effacing Sita of the Ramayana epic. This Mother figure of Dalit women controls her own sexuality and is the conferrer of life and death. She is therefore an important figure in the process of women's awakening to self-esteem, as is frequently noted by Goddess scholars.[26]

Dalit women do not only sing of the Mother goddesses, but also include and sometimes re-shape those from the Hindu pantheon. One woman remarked that even neo-Buddhists have no problem worshipping Hindu goddesses! Older songs can be re-shaped and given a Christian meaning. In this delightful song Christ's own mother is asked to let her child come:

> There are wheels and tops in my house,
> O affectionate Mother.
> Give me the player of toys, O affectionate Mother.
> There are yellow kites in my house, O affectionate Mother.
> Give me the flyer of kites, O affectionate Mother.[27]

24. Franco *et al.*, *The Silken Swing*, p. 205.
25. Franco *et al.*, *The Silken Swing*, p. 207.
26. See Carol Christ, *The Rebirth of the Goddess* (New York: Addison-Wesley Publishing Co., 1997).)
27. Franco *et al.*, *The Silken Swing*, p. 209.

In addition to these types of songs, dances and stories, there are others more directly related to subversion and social transformation.[28] First, Gabriele Dietrich relates how deviant women who have met a violent end can become village goddesses. The goddess Mariammal began life as an abandoned child.

> A washerwoman had found her and handed her over to Varuna raja who brought her up as Renuka Parameshwari. Renuka was married to a saint, Jama – dagni. Her chastity was such that she could carry water in an imaginary pot.[29]

However, this capacity was lost when, one day, she became enchanted by the reflection of Arjuna in the water. When her angry husband commanded his son Parasuram to kill his mother, Renuka sought refuge in the house of a Dalit woman. Alas, in the fight that followed, Parasuram beheaded both women! Later he craved a boon from his father, and asked for his mother's life. But, confused, he put the head of Renuka on the Dalit woman's body, and the Dalit head of the Parayar woman on the body of Renuka. Then the woman with the Brahmin head and the Dalit body became Mariammal, the goddess of smallpox, while the woman with the Dalit head and the Brahmin body became Ellaiyammal, the goddess of boundaries.

Both these goddesses are very popular in Dalit localities. I have told this story in full because of the symbolism it displays of subversion and oppression, especially of transgression of caste boundaries – and also because of the importance of these goddesses, referred to earlier as Mariyamman and Ellaiyamman of the Paraiyars of Tamil Nadu. This creative subversion of myths is an important strand in the spirituality of Dalits and in particular, Dalit women. The independence of Dalit goddesses must be stressed. They are a-sexual, Sathianathan Clarke notes, free from the pursuit of male gods:

---

28. For more information on songs, particularly 'Insult' songs at weddings and feasts, see Gloria Goodwin Raheja and Anne Grodzins Gold, *Listen to the Heron's Words* (Berkeley, CA: University of California Press, 1994).

29. Gabriele Dietrich, 'Subversion, Transgression, Transcendence – "Asian Spirituality in the light of Dalit and Adivasi Struggles"', in Gabriele Dietrich, *A New Thing on Earth: Hopes and Fears Facing Feminist Theology* (Delhi: ISPK for TTS, Madurai, 2001), pp. 245–46.

They are overseers of procreation and protection, but the working out of their own sexual passion and fertility is not the subject of Paraiyar theological discourse.[30]

These goddesses also express symbolic power as icons of resistance. Clarke explains this clearly with reference to Ellaiyamman.[31] He says that this goddess is 'the axis of the Paraiyar religion,' arguing etymologically that in Tamil 'ellam' means 'all', making her 'mother of all'. In the colony of Malaipallam she is referred to as 'Mother of all beings' and as 'the eldest sister of all the manifestations of shakti.'[32] She exhibits the sexual independence referred to earlier. (In fact both goddesses, Ellaiyamman and Mariyamman, once they became deities, became independent of their past relationships). But equally significantly, 'ellai' means 'boundary,' making the goddess mother of the boundaries, believed to protect the inhabitants of the colony from disease, disaster and famine. Clarke sees Ellaiyamman as an iconic representation of resistance to the world of the caste Hindu:

> She shields and polices the geographic, social and cultural space of the Paraiyar from the continuous colonising proclivity of the caste people.[33]

In the procession of the yearly festival she is taken to the borders in every direction and a sacrifice is performed in order to energize her power. One interpretation for her standing at the boundaries, one that specifically affects women, is that she stands as a warning to those who may caste an 'evil eye' on the people – especially the women and children.

These accounts focus on goddesses in Tamil Nadu. Similar stories are told of goddesses in Andhra Pradesh. Kancha Ilaiah tells of the most popular goddess, Pochamamma:

> The people can approach her without the medium of a priest. They talk to the goddess as they talk among themselves. "Mother," they say, "we have seeded the fields, now you must ensure that

30. Sathianathan Clarke, *Dalits and Christianity: Subaltern Religion and Liberation Theology in India* (Delhi: Oxford University Press, 1998), p. 72.

31. Clarke, *Dalits and Christianity*, pp. 100–101.

32. Clarke, *Dalits and Christianity*.

33. Clarke, *Dalits and Christianity*, p. 102.

34. Kancha Ilaiah, *Why I am not a Hindu: A Sudra Critique of Hindutva, Philosophy, Culture and Political Economy* (Calcutta: Samya, 2002 [1996]), pp. 91–100.

the crop grows well, one of our children is sick – it is your bounded duty to cure her...[34]

Pochamamma is in tune with her peoples' lives and greatest concerns – crops, sickness and reproduction. Her approachability is typical of Dalit goddesses. As Sister Shalini remarks:

Dalitbahujan society never allowed the emergence of a priestly class/caste that is alienated from production and alienates the Goddesses and Gods from the people.[35]

That this would have severe consequences for Christian Dalit women must be discussed later.

But male deities can also offer hope of resistance and subversion. A story is told of the sixteenth century saint Ravi Das, recounted by *Regar* women of Rajasthan. (Regars – who were cited in Chapter 2 – were traditionally leatherworkers, – *chamars* elsewhere – but nowadays have long since ceased having anything to do with dead animals and their hides).[36] For these Regar women what was important about Ravi Dass was that, as a baby, he had first refused to suckle from his Untouchable mother's breast, but did so after the midwife's instruction to:

Drink mother's milk; wherever you were born you are born, so drink happily; your name will be worshipped, you will be famed, no matter in which community you were born.[37]

This particular community of Regar women had a profusion of stories about Ravi Das, (or Raidas) especially in connection with the Goddess Ganga (river Ganges). A particularly dramatic story takes place at a wedding feast, where a *thakur*, or high-caste land-owner attempts to marry the goddess. The denouement comes when the Goddess makes the water from the tanning pit overflow, and washes away the whole wedding party! So, even though there are mixed messages here, as Grodzins Gold observes – 'God loves me as I am', versus 'God will bring down the mighty from their seat' – the stories and songs cited here give ample material to show that Dalit women are far from passive victims amidst all the

35. Sister Shalini, unpublished paper, p. 10, ref. 26.
36. See, Grodzins Gold and Gujar, *In the Time of Trees and Sorrows*, pp. 93, 206–207.
37. Grodzins Gold and Gujar, *In the Time of Trees and Sorrows*, p. 207.
38. Although it is said that he removed some of her prophetic power by co-opting her in his own freedom struggle: see Chapter 8 and the discussion of tensions between Gandhi and Ambedkar.

suffering heaped upon them: they are capable of practising irony and subversion within the system as well as taking steps to transgress its boundaries.

Mirabai – A Subversive Figure

Within the genre of devotional songs as bringing hope of subversion and transgression of boundaries, the fifteenth century saint, Mira, deserves a special place. Mira, much later than Janabai (cited at the beginning of the chapter) is a relative latecomer to the Bhakti, or devotional movement. Mira *Bhajans* or hymns are very popular, especially with women. (Even Gandhi admired her for her courageous stance in leaving an oppressive situation and overcoming poverty through her creativity and wanted her hymns sung in his Ashrams).[38] It is particularly Mira's overturning of polluted relationships and her acceptance of a Chamar man, Rohidas, as her guru that enables the assertion of caste status as having moral power.[39]

Mira lived in Chittoor in Rajasthan, (which was to become part of the kingdom of Mewar). Chittoor was the original capital. Her devotion to Krishna and the strength of his love enabled her to reject not only the authority of her husband, the ruler of Chittoor, but the whole militarist, caste-ridden society. Dietrich relates:

> Mirabai, opting out of the privileged life at the court of Chittoor, had to cope with attempts to murder her and was facing social ostracism.[40]

Here is how Mira writes of her heart's desire:

> It is raining in the month of Savan,
> I like the rain coming down.
> In Savan my heart starts to pine,
> I hear the sound of Hari coming.
> The clouds have rolled in from all sides,
> Lightning occurs and it pours.
> Tiny drops come from the clouds,
> And I enjoy the cool breeze,
> O Lord of Mira, called Giradhar Nagar,
> The cloudy season is for singing joyfully.[41]

39. Franco *et al.*, *The Silken Swing*, p. 210.
40. Dietrich, 'The Relationship Between Women's Movement and Dalit Movements', p. 133.
41. The source is http://www.cs.colostate.edu/-malaiya/mira.htm

As has been related, because of her *chamar* guru and her oral tradition of songs, which became a medium of expression for alternative values for poor people of all castes as well as Dalits, Mira's influence carries on to this day. She is the inspiration for a group of underprivileged people linked with each other through affirming and living a simple life uncorrupted by wealth and privilege. This inspiration is a means of challenging both patriarchal and caste values and can open up the way to a different social vision. Despite such subversive sources, and sustenance of earth-based rituals, the prevailing picture of the religion of Dalit women remains ambiguous, because of its intrinsic link with patriarchy and oppressive elements of Hinduism.

But in its socially subversive elements there are similarities with the struggles of the early Christians and the Jesus movement, and it is to Christianity that we now turn.

Chapter 6

Dalit Women, Christianity and Christian Church

> The contemporary literature, including even women's missionary magazines were amazingly silent about Dalit women. A break with the past was extremely difficult for them because their lives, even more than the men's, were totally absorbed by the constant pre-dawn to dark drudgery of survival – John Webster[1]

This chapter does not attempt to give a comprehensive history of the origins of the Dalit Christian Church but to try to break the silence of this history as regards women, a silence encountered in this area as in others. How to penetrate the silence surrounding the experiences of Dalit women in the Christian Church is the hope. I attempt this first, through seeking a context for the emergence of Christianity in India and to understand why Dalits should want to convert to a faith which has scant claim to be indigenous or gives evidence that their situation would be transformed. I explore the reasons for the lack of conversion success that Christian missionaries have experienced, before turning to more recent developments, thus paving the way for the emergence of Dalit Liberation Theology, discussed in the next Chapter as Dalit Feminist Liberation Theology.

Seeking a Context for Indian Christianity

James Massey suggests that out of India's 20m Christians, about 11m are Dalits. In some states the percentage is higher: in his own state, the Punjab, for example, the percentage of Christians is 95 percent.[2] Some suggest a higher figure – that between 75 percent and 80 percent of Christians are Dalits, about 14m. But in any case, 60 percent of all Catholics in India are Dalits.

---

1. John Webster, *The Dalit Christians: A History* (New Delhi: ISPCK, 1992), p. 69.
2. James Massey, *The Struggle of India's Dalits for Identity, Solidarity and Liberation* (Geneva: World Council of Churches Publications, 1997), p. 65.

Christianity has an ancient heritage in India: the Apostle Thomas is said to have brought Christian faith to (what is now) Kerala in 52ce. Little is known about these early Christian communities, but when the Portuguese arrived in 1498, they found a well-established community in the region.[3] These Syrian Christians considered themselves to be descended from St Thomas, whose tomb is believed to be in San Thome Cathedral in Old Chennai (Madras). A very unedifying struggle then ensued wherein the Syrian Church was forced to accept the authority of Rome, specifically the authority of the Pope – thus ending their obedience to the Patriarch. The Portuguese had an active conversion policy and some Dalits were then converted. From the outset there was an issue about integrating Dalits within the existing caste community, a problem that became intensified, and remains a troubling issue to this day – with the attempts of the seventeenth century Jesuit Missionary, Fr Robert de Nobili, who came to India in 1608. His ascetic lifestyle and teaching appealed to the Brahmin *sannyasi*, or holy men, who, on conversion to Christianity, then ministered to the higher castes. In general de Nobili allowed caste distinctions to remain in his mission and the Catholic Church in general worked within the caste system, almost seeing its social organization as a given. This could be one reason why the Christian percentage in India has never grown beyond around 4 percent, (2 percent is the figure in many states) and is often considered almost to be a foreign implant. Another reason given by Dr Ambedkar himself was that Indians associated Christianity with its representatives within the East India Company: these had a widespread reputation for drunkenness and immorality. Gandhi was not impressed by the representative of Christianity he met and cited this as one reason why he did not become a Christian!

The Papal Bull of 1623, in response to Fr Robert de Nobili, acceded to the request of the missionaries to accommodate themselves to certain caste practices and customs of the new converts.[4] Later Protestant missionaries in general had a better reputation and from the outset, in the nineteenth century, seem to have included the lower castes and outcastes in their preaching and missionary activity. Mass movements to Christianity in the Punjab and in different parts of India, were led by Dalit leaders:

3. Webster, *The Dalit Christians*, pp. 34–35.
4. S. Lourdeswamy, *Empowerment of Dalit Christians* (New Delhi: Centre for Dalit/Subaltern Studies, 2005), p. 35.

James Massey tells the story of Ditt, in the Punjab, a dealer in hides, who was baptised in 1873 and in the 11 years after his Baptism had brought more than 500 people into Christianity.[5]

Yet, as we shall see, even if Christianity remains a small percentage within the religious situation in India, and in many places is a middle-class phenomenon, conversion to Christianity for Dalits has had many positive outcomes.

Why did Dalits convert in such large numbers? Gandhi considered these conversions as 'conversion of convenience' and declared that Dalits were incapable of understanding the Christian message or evaluating it in relation to other alternatives. His most unfortunate statement was:

> Would you preach the Gospel to a cow? Well, some of the Untouchables are worse than cows in understanding. I mean that they can no more distinguish between the relative merits of Islam and Hinduism and Christianity than a cow.[6]

This statement, although written in a specific context, appears to grossly undervalue the conversion movement. (And we must acknowledge that Gandhi's own thoughts matured: this statement must not be taken as evidence against his abhorrence towards the practice of Untouchability and his determination to reform it).

For Dalits, conversion to Christianity through the missionaries from the seventeenth century onwards was entered on in the hope of breaking free from the caste system, and encountering the reality of the liberating news of the Gospel of Jesus Christ. They wished to regain dignity and equality, to experience solidarity in times of suffering, and to gain upward mobility by getting education and economic privileges.[7] There are many Gospel stories of the transforming effect of hearing stories of Jesus, the poor and rejected suffering man, the promises that God would raise up the poor and lowly and caste down the powerful and mighty – and these stories had a great impact on both women and men.

5. James Massey, *Down-Trodden: The Struggle of India's Dalits for Identity, Solidarity and Liberation* (Geneva: World Council of Churches Publications, 1997), pp. 65–66.

6. Cited in John C.B. Webster, *Religion and Dalit Liberation* (New Delhi: Manohar, 2002), p. 57. He is quoting from M.K. Gandhi, *Christian Missions: Their Place in India* (Ahmedabad: Navajivan Press, 1941). This was written after Ambedkar's declaration that he would leave Hinduism – see Chapter 8.

7. Lourdeswamy, *Empowerment of Dalit Christians*, pp. 34–35.

Many missionaries report a great change in consciousness among Dalit people, a growth of self-esteem, and a breaking free from the sense of being stigmatized, even if the immediate effect for many was to worsen their economic condition owing to backlash from the local caste communities.

But, as Samuel Jayakumar concluded, the Christian missionaries certainly contributed to an awakening of consciousness for Dalit communities, as well as many practical, positive outcomes.[8] Christianity offered the promise of a new and alternate society; the introduction of the vernacular liturgy and, from the specific perspective of this book, this education also offered a transforming potential for women:

> Female education brought dignity to future wives and mothers. For the outcastes, their new religious identity, that is, the association with Christ and fellow believers had a precedence over communal identity. They slowly learnt to live as a family and the family of God.[9]

A key figure binding the local community to the Christian Church was the catechist-teacher. This man (it appears to have been usually a man):

> alone from day to day bears the burden of the work through good report and ill. It is he who teaches all the children during the week, and who preaches on Sunday. Whoever falls sick in the village, it is he who will be looked to for advice, healing and prayers.... In oppressions by the caste people, in dominant joys and sorrows, in disputes as to ownership of land, or as to village right of way, this teacher-catechist is called to be the guide, philosopher and friend of the community...[10]

But, to Christianity's shame, caste-based discrimination followed the Dalit people even into the Christian Church and continues to this day.

Added to this injustice, at this point in history, Christians, both women and men are denied by the Indian government the constitutional privileges given to other Dalits – a grave international human rights issue. That is the political situation, justified because

8. Samuel Jayakumar, *Dalit Consciousness and Christian Conversion* (New Delhi: ISPCK, 1999), pp. 217–21.

9. Jayakumar, *Dalit Consciousness*, p. 218.

10. Godfrey E. Phillips, *The Outcastes' Hope or Work Among the Depressed Classes in India* (London: Baptist Missionary Society, 1915) p. 68.

Christianity is not considered to be authentically Indian and therefore undeserving of the same political privileges as Hindu and Muslim Dalits.

Within the church itself caste segregation during worship, and especially in the taking of Holy Communion, is often practised. As stated, there are about 20m Christians in India – estimates vary – and yet not even 8 percent of the Dalit community are represented in the Church's hierarchy (whether Protestant or Roman Catholic). Nor is this only an issue for India. Caste oppression – as I have noted, is experienced by Dalits in Pakistan, Bangladesh and Nepal, and even follows Dalits to Britain. Not that it is easy for a Dalit Christian woman to visit Britain at all: there is tremendous pressure to exclude Dalit applications for study possibilities (especially if they are women) and to give these to caste Christians.[11] Another area of criticism is that Dalits who converted to Christianity often used the new opportunities presented for their own personal advantage:

> Many members of my own caste have become Christians and most of them do not recommend Christianity to the remainder of us. Some have gone to boarding schools and have enjoyed high privilege. We think of them as high products of your missionary efforts and what sort of people are they? Selfish and self-centred. They don't care a snap of their finger what becomes of their former caste associates so long as they and their families, or they and the little group who have become Christians, get ahead. Indeed, their chief concern with reference to their old caste associates is to hide the fact that they were ever in the same community.[12]

This complaint flags up a frequent cri de coeur, that Christian missionaries often favoured the élite, or middle-class, who were quick to respond to the educational advantages they offered.

The Experience of Dalit Women within Christianity

Can one find any glimpses as to how the conversion process affected and changed women? Often the experience of Dalit women as Christians to a large extent simply repeats their socialization into

11. My sources for this story are personal and cannot be named.
12. J. Wasdom Pickett, *Christ's Way to India's Heart* (Lucknow: Lucknow Publishing House, 1938), pp. 22–23.

inferiority. Women have also had to encounter the deep ambiguity – putting it at its best! – of Christian theology towards women and to female sexuality. Although in some of the early (missionary) conversion stories there is evidence of women's leadership, after 1947 there was a transfer of power to the urban Christian elite and women largely lost this initiative. Caste Christianity (the focus of this work insofar as it affects women), increases the separation of the Dalit people from caste Christians in general and women's discrimination in particular. Stories of segregation in Church are often repeated. A recent story from Tamil Nadu reported the shock of a young, zealous priest on arriving at a church, only to find a wall in the centre of the nave, separating caste-Christians from Dalits. When he removed the wall he was murdered by a powerful group of caste Christians.[13] Fr Lourduswamy, in his book *Towards Empowerment of Dalit Christians*, gives a comprehensive account of discrimination of Dalits in Christian Churches throughout India.[14]

According to Sister Shalini, a Roman Catholic sister, in a story that reflects the earlier one of the rural women in Uttar Pradesh, this is the reality:

> Dalit women long for dignity and respect in society and in the church. Being economically poor and being Dalits they feel excluded and discriminated. "When we go to meet the parish priest," says Sahaya Mary, "Father does not even ask us to sit down".[15]

Further, this particular parish in Chennai where Sister Shalini Mulakal conducted her research, operates on caste lines: the Basic Christian Communities (BCCs) that in Latin America operate as grass roots solidarity amongst the poorer people work here in a discriminatory way. A monthly fee is demanded for Church membership. And the whole thrust on the spiritual dimension of faith observance ignores the desperate economic poverty of the Dalit community. Lancy Lobo refers to:

13. Confidential anonymous source.

14. S. Lourdeswamy, *Toward Empowerment of Dalit Christians: Equal Rights to All Dalits* (New Delhi: Centre for Dalit/Subaltern Studies, 2005).

15. Sister Shalini Mulakal, 'Hunger for Food and Thirst for Dignity: Well-being as Hermeneutical Key to a Feminist Soteriology,' Unpublished paper based on the author's research into the Catholic parish of Thiruvetriyur, a suburb of Chennai, formerly Madras.

the disinterest of clergy in social matters such as unemployment, poverty, drought, corruption and political misrule. In such structural matters they stay away and do relief and service. They ask the people to pray to Jesus. Prayer is preferred to social awareness.[16]

Not only is the lack of engagement with structural issues a problem. Simply approaching the priest is fraught with difficulties. Dalit women were heard to say here that it was easier to approach a goddess than a Christian priest! The approachability of the goddesses within Dalit Spirituality by comparison with religions where male priestly castes dominate is a striking fact. But all these difficulties must be placed within the wider context of the way the Christian church has dealt with caste issues. A huge failure to engage with the life struggles of lower castes and Dalits in particular, let alone challenge the system is remarked on by most of the sources. Like all the issues this book addresses, this impacts worse on women.

Yet, in other places, research offers some positive messages. The work of John Webster and his team – also in the Chennai (Madras) area – shows how the stories of the love and compassion of Jesus and the courage of some of the biblical women offer new hope to Dalit women.[17] The Bible began to be read by them in a new way, as I shall explore in the following chapter. Giving women access to the text is itself a liberating step. The cultivation of a life of prayer was also experienced as giving inner strength to women. Further, when Webster's team examined the comparative practices around childbirth among Christian and 'Hindu' Dalits, they found that where the practices were almost identical, there was less girl infanticide among Christian women as well as a stronger sense of self-esteem in younger Dalit Christian mothers. This must be sign of hope for the future.

Another hopeful experience that Webster uncovered gives very positive indications:

The poor rural women have appropriated those stories, images and meanings which relate God's loving care directly to their

16. Lancy Lobo, 'Visions, Illusions and Dilemmas of Dalit Christians in India,' in Ghanshysam Shah (ed.), *Dalit Identity and Politics: Cultural Subordination and the Dalit Challenge*, Vol. 2 (New Delhi: Sage Publications, 2001), pp. 242–57, quotation p. 254.

17. John Webster, Deborah Premraj, Ida Swamidos, Rashilda Udayakumar, Chandra Yesuratnam, *From Role to Identity: Dalit Christian Women in Transition* (New Delhi: ISPCK, 1997).

own or their family's struggles to survive with a measure of dignity in the face of suffering and adversity. The urban lower (middle) class women have appropriated those which relate to their own and their family's respectability in a society which tends to deny them that. What both have in common is the (basically unstated) conviction that the God they worship combines both masculine and feminist qualities; that in this God's view all people – women and men as well as Dalits and non-Dalits – are equal; and that prayer is at the very heart of religious life.[18]

Yet another study by a research team from St Xavier's College, Ahmedabad, in a specific area of Gujarat where female infanticide is widely practiced, shows Dalit Christians as practicing a much lower rate of girl infanticide compared with Hindu and tribal women.[19] The same study points to the influence of religious sisters on Dalit women: their convent was regarded as a place of welcome and hospitality, offering an important *safe space* for women to meet. This is without estimating the enormous activist contributions of some communities of religious sisters in struggling with Dalit women for justice, for example, in the area of child prostitution and trafficking. Yet Christian education, a cherished route out of oppression, could provide a further site of misery. The story of Bama, a poor Dalit woman, who was very intelligent, illustrates this ambiguity. Bama was advised by her brother to pursue higher education:

> Because we are born into the Paraya jati, we are never given any honour or dignity or respect. We are stripped of all that. But if we study and make progress, we can throw away these indignities. So study with care, learn all you can. If you are always ahead in your lessons, people will come to you of their own accord and attach themselves to you. Work hard and learn.[20]

Bama took this advice to heart, studied for BA and B.Ed degrees, enduring the humiliations that came her way 'with a combination of shame and anger.'[21] Although the Catholic Church provided the

---

18. Webster, Premraj *et al.*, *From Role to Identity*, p. 107.

19. Fernando Franco, Jyotsna Macwan, Suguna Ramanathan (eds), *The Silken Swing: The Cultural Universe of Dalit Women* (Calcutta: Stree, 2000).

20. Bama, *Karukka* (trans. Laxmi Homstrom; Chennai: Macmillan, 2000), p. 15.

21. As John Webster relates, *Religion and Dalit Liberation* (Delhi: Manohar, 2002), p. 128.

schools giving her opportunities for an education, and the inspiration
to become a nun, she found the nuns and priests so full of caste
prejudice that she left the order. But she was so damaged by the
experience that it was almost impossible to live in the real world:

> At the time I entered the convent, I was like the strong core of a
> teak tree. Both in mind and in body I was as firm and steadfast
> as that. But when I came out, I had lost all my strength, and was
> as feeble as a *murunga* tree that blows over in the wind. It was
> only after I entered the convent that I fell prey to every illness
> and disease. My mind, too, had been buffeted and knocked about,
> so that I was only living a half-life or a quarter-life.[22]

Eventually, however, she was able to adjust and move slowly
forward, step by step.

Even though the ground level experience is fraught with the
difficulties I have described, it has to be said that the Catholic
hierarchy, as well as the Churches of North and South India have
issued statements regularly condemning caste discrimination, well
aware that it stands in flagrant contradiction to the Christian
Gospel.[23] The Christian Churches have in addition consistently
campaigned for Equal Constitutional Rights for Dalit Christians.
The response of the government has been to give assurances that
have never been fulfilled.

The Contribution of Dalit Theologians

What can be said – within this rather contradictory picture I have
presented – is that, despite the opposition of upper-caste Christians,
and a government unwilling to rock the boat, the missionaries and
the Church in general have tried to improve the lot of the Dalit
people. Second, the context has been gradually changing. As well
as some of the reform movements – which will be mentioned later
– in the Christian Church, the liberation movements of Latin America
and elsewhere have had a great influence on the theology of Dalits
themselves.

So the key contributions of some inspiring theologians is worthy
of mention. The late A.P. Nirmal is regarded with great respect,
almost as the father of Dalit Theology. His early death in 1995 is

22. Cited in Webster, *Religion and Dalit Liberation*, p. 130.
23. See Fr Lourduswamy, *Towards Empowerment of Dalit Christians* (New
Delhi: Centre for Dalit/Subaltern Studies 2005) pp. 51–67.

greatly mourned. Dalit theology can be regarded as an indigenous form of Liberation Theology, even if it has not always been seen as that, submerged as it can be within a general struggle against poverty that can obscure the distinctive situation of Dalits.

Nirmal's theology used the category of *pathos* as starting point: *pathos*, suffering, is the default position of the Dalit people. Linking with the Isaiahan image of the suffering Servant, Jesus is understood as the primordial Dalit, sharing their suffering, with a hopeful mission to the oppressed that this suffering may be transcended.[24] This is still proving an inspiring and helpful category. For example, there are now research students using this as a category in their constructive Dalit Theologies. (Charles Singaram, from Tamil Nadu, recently grounded his PhD thesis on Dalit Theology on the concept of the *pathos* of both Christ and the Dalit people).[25]

Nirmal showed clearly the problem of Indian Christian Theology as idealizing the caste-system and as growing out of missionary attitudes and approaches to caste. A further chapter questions why Dalit theology has to a certain extent stagnated and why it has never developed a systematic approach. This chapter in fact lays the ground for the final presentation of a systematic Dalit Theology in showing how already in Nirmal's work, *pathos* is privileged over *praxis*.

Another influential theologian is Fr Anthony Raj, who recommended a sociological foundation for Dalit Theology: Dalits can only be free by an active responsible disobedience.[26] The late Dr Abraham Ayrookuzheil took seriously the powerlessness of Dalits. He suggested creating for Dalits a counter-culture to the caste-oriented society, drawing power from Dalit culture for their own liberation. One of the most pastorally oriented Dalit theologians is Masilmani Azariah, Bishop of Chennai since 1990. As one key commentator wrote:

> Azaraiah's writings bring together a number of themes that are characteristic of Dalit theology; the need to rewrite history from a Dalit perspective, the rape of their culture, traditions and dignity

24. Arvind P. Nirmal (ed.), *A Reader in Dalit Theology* (Chennai: Gurukul Lutheran Theological College, 1989).

25. Charles Singaram, University of Birmingham PhD thesis, December 2004.

26. This paragraph is a paraphrase of Masilamani Azariah, *A Pastor's Search for Dalit Theology* (Chennai: ISPCK, 2000), pp. 183–85.

by Aryan conquest and Brahmanical priestcraft, the
institutionalised poverty of the bottom quarter of India's
population, the necessity of awakening the conscience to break
free from the stranglehold of a slave mentality.[27]

All these attempts to create a Dalit Liberation Theology are of
value for Dalit Christians. There can be no doubt that these writers
are determined to oppose caste discrimination and see it as
contradictory to the Christian Gospel. They are also important in
the slow process of consciousness-raising and transforming the
internalizing of oppression mentality that has prevented Dalits from
mobilizing for their own liberation. And third, they are instrumental
in the way the Churches have begun to work with Dalit communities
especially in the city slums. The Delhi Brotherhood is one
outstanding example of a Christian Religious Congregation working
with Dalit children in the slums using a Liberation theology-inspired
method.

Yet hardly any theologian seems able to show gender sensitivity
and awareness of the way that caste discrimination affects and
scars women more deeply than men, and allows them few escape
routes. This follows a widespread pattern of traditional Christian
theology that has, until recently, been blind to its own patriarchal
structures. Without confronting patriarchy in society and in religious
organizations, teachings and ethics, its insidious ability to shore-up
caste-ism will not be uncovered. The one exception to this situation
that I have been able to discover is the Centre for Dalit/Subaltern
Studies in New Delhi, whose Director is Professor James Massey.
He and his team – whose work is not purely academic, since they
run many practical projects in Delhi slums – are well aware of the
problems I have outlined. They make many attempts to bring women
into their team and theological endeavours. But for many reasons –
some of which have been outlined – they have not as yet been
successful.

Conclusion

In conclusion, it can be said that the positive role of the Churches
for women has been, first, up to the present day to offer education
as a gateway to further opportunities to Dalit girls and women,

27. Cited in Azariah, *A Pastor's Search*, pp. 185–86.

even though it has taken courage and persistence to endure the humiliation and bullying that may occur in Church institutions. Second, the life of faith itself has proved a great resource for developing inner strength and resourcefulness. Third, the Churches have frequently offered safe spaces which are key to understanding how Dalit women negotiate areas of freedom in their lives. (Other spaces for women's interaction are while collecting water and fodder – of course these may be far from safe! – going for ablutions, social occasions and festivals).[28]

This chapter has opened up many areas in the religious lives of Dalit women within Christianity. An ambiguous picture has been presented: there are areas of hope and dreams of freedom – yet areas of great suffering and discrimination on many counts have been revealed. For example, the Church respects motherhood and the family, of central importance to Dalit women, yet may turn a blind eye to the suffering of many Dalit women within the family, and to the fact that she may be subjected to the violence of her husband. Leadership within all the churches is still a problem for Dalit women.[29]

The greatest obstacle to progress in the lives of Dalit women is the lack of gender sensitivity and awareness even of the most well-meaning leaders and theologians. Many Dalit women have become conscious of new possibilities offered by education and are involved in both political and religious struggles. Others still see no possibilities of social change, and remain locked in the prison of discrimination and many-levelled oppression, although they may still make every use of religious festivity, song, myth or poem to make life more bearable within the system. The urgent task is to attempt some theological analysis that may offer women more hope.

28. Franco *et al.*, *The Silken Swing*, p. 113.
29. This is equally true for many Churches in the West, such as Roman Catholic and Orthodox Churches.

Chapter 7

DALIT WOMEN AND FEMINIST LIBERATION THEOLOGY

Doing women's theology in India calls for an adequate theological
method that would undertake a critical analysis of all major
structures of oppression, the interconnectedness of these structures
as well as the legitimising of ideology ...Within the Christian
fold the association between caste and patriarchy is established
by the fact that it is the caste (ethnic) churches which are opposed
to the ordination of women – V. Devasahayam[1]

The Dalit Struggle Becomes an International Issue

One of the principles of Liberation Theology is that not only does it
address specific oppression in context, but that the victims are the
rightful agents of their own liberation. Empowerment and agency
of the victims themselves in the process is vital: well-meaning
'liberators' should not act on their behalf, but stand with them in
an effective solidarity. This is what has been happening with the
Dalit Movement. Because Dalits have felt betrayed by the leaders
of the caste system, they have appealed to the world at large to
work with them for justice. There are key landmarks in this process:
in 1999 the Human Rights Watch Report, 'Broken People: Caste
Violence against India's Untouchables,' was published.[2] In 2001,
there was a strong Dalit presence at the United Nations World
Conference against Racism. This then led to the presence at the
2003 Asian Social Forum, in Hyderabad, Andhra Pradesh, of nearly
1,000 Dalit representatives of 25 organizations, in India and 17 from
overseas. The biggest event of this kind that attracted most
international attention must be reckoned the World Social Forum

1. V. Devasahayam, *Doing Dalit Theology in Biblical Key* (Gurukul: ISPCK,
1997), p. 30.
2. See Series Editors' Note to Hugo Gorringe, *Untouchable Citizens: Dalit
Movements and Democratisation in Tamil Nadu* (New Delhi: Sage Publications
India, 2005), pp. 11–12.

at Mumbai in 2004 which met in opposition to the World Economic Forum, because of its commitment to liberalization and privatization. James Massey described this dramatic event:

> Massive show of strength by the social activists, intellectuals, artists, workers, weaker sections, minorities, Dalits, adivasis, tribals, youths, women, children, differently abled people, sex workers and older people...They came from more than a hundred countries around the world. Every day the voices of more than a 100,000 victims were heard from marches, conferences, rallies, public meetings, seminars, workshops and cultural shows.[3]

Though undeniably an event with potential for maximum impact, Massey questions what was actually achieved. Local people living near the venue were apparently unaware of what was happening, let alone its significance. Undeniably many groups achieved a profile on a very wide scale, (5,000 groups had participated), and the interaction between them was very fruitful, stimulating and informative. The actual theme of the Forum was 'another World is possible' and its two pillars were 'social justice' and 'genuine democracy'. Another focus was the impact of neo-liberalization in creating a vulnerable underclass. All these issues were key ones for Dalits.[4] But major speakers like Arundhati Roy and Medha Patkar, (both activists in the Sardar Sarovar Dam campaign), while rightly criticizing the Iraq War, and condemning capitalist imperialism and neo-liberalism, failed to address Dalit issues with any force.[5] It is true that Dalit NGO's presented workshops, seminars, non-stop films on Dalit issues, and there was an immense variety of cultural programmes, but somehow Dalits failed to get their own agenda understood as of major importance to the Forum as a whole. Even the former President of India, Mr K.R. Narayanan, himself from a Dalit background, while speaking on the ill-effects of globalization, failed to connect these with the Dalit situation.

Yet the participation of women has to be seen as one of the successes. On a practical level, it was experienced as a unique holiday:

> For 6 days they did not worry about cooking, cleaning, fetching water and fodder, taking care of the elderly and serving their

3. James Massey, '*The Dalit Presence at the World Social Forum 2004*' in T.K. John (ed.), *Broken Among the Victims: Dalit Presence at the World Social Forum 2004* (New Delhi: Centre for Dalit/Subaltern Studies, 2004), p. 102.

4. This has been noted in Chapter 1.

5. Massey, '*The Dalit Presence,*' pp. 110–11.

husbands...They were found singing and dancing, raising slogans and protesting, listening to other groups and participating in seminars and workshops, testifying to the violence and abuse they were subjected to.[6]

For the first time, many women found a voice to express their problems of their own lives, especially those around violence and sexual humiliation. It became clear to participants that the situation of Dalit women was deteriorating. And even if on the level of major strategy there appeared to be few outcomes, at grassroots level, many alliances between groups were made and plans to network were agreed on. For a few days women were given a taste of an alternative world.[7] That Dalit women's issues had achieved international limelight is shown by the fact that a number of meetings have taken place, the most notable of which was The Hague Convention on the Rights of Dalit Women in 2006 – referred to Chapter 3.

The Social Forum example is illustrative of some of the difficulties encountered in trying to achieve effective solidarity at an international level, essential step though this is. Another drawback in envisaging a Feminist Liberation Theology in the Dalit Asian context is that, though there are millions of Dalit Christians, Christians throughout India form a low percentage of the population – ranging from 2 percent to 5 percent in some areas. Even the vocabulary of theology has Christian overtones and may be counterproductive in some areas. So, first, many Christian groups have learnt to be humble, inclusive and pluralist in their working methods in such a context; second, the church has an international outreach and access to financial and educational resources that can be harnessed for liberation,[8] and finally, Dalit feminist theology will be multi-dimensional in the strengths it draws on, reaching beyond the boundaries of Christian theology both to Dalit spiritualities and to secular movements as well as the solidarity of NGO's.

---

6. Sister Shalini Mulakal, 'WSF 2004: A Feminist Perspective', in T.K. John (ed.), *Broken Among the Victims*, , pp. 116–28.

7. Mulakal, 'WSF 2004,' p. 128.

8. As mentioned in the last chapter.

Dalit Feminist Liberation Theology: Getting off the Ground

First, there needs to be clarity as to some of the difficulties. I have already referred to the low self-esteem of many Dalit women, and the internalization of inferiority imposed on her by the caste system, that can actually form deep psychic intergenerational wounds. Dalit Women's Movements take this very seriously. But there are further obstacles. Because of the heavy burden of daily practical work and child care, women find it very hard even to attend the meetings necessary for political organization and action. Her husband may not even allow her to participate. There is certainly no extra free time for the kinds of conversations helpful to strategize. This is a key issue not only for poor women:

> "Can we stand at a tea-shop and drink tea?" Viji, a lecturer at the college, asked. "Can a hardworking woman coming back from her work stand at a tea-shop, and have a drink? Imagine the reaction!" "Look at her! What effrontery!"... So what are these spaces for? Certainly not for us![9]

The fact that in public meetings, women and men sit apart is also a problem to be overcome. In many village meetings I have attended in Rajasthan, veiled women have sat in silence in the background, while men discussed issues that affected them directly. It is not only the presence of men, but the fact that younger, more active women may be effectively muzzled because of the presence of a mother-in-law, or another dominant female personality. But these are problems that can be overcome through the unwavering commitment of a local NGO. Once I was present at conference on drought, in the Thar Desert, (north of Jodhpur), and was amazed by the eloquence of a young woman speaker. I was told she had been an elected representative to the Village Development Council, but prevented by her husband from going to meetings. She persisted, helped by the local NGO, *Gravis*.[10] Each time she went, she was beaten by him on her return home. But she persisted and eventually found courage to speak. But no one listened to her! Still she persisted and finally her wisdom, courage and eloquence won through. When I saw her, even the influential elders were listening in respect! Such women become vital role models for other women.

9. Hugo Gorringe, *Untouchable Citizens*, p. 233.
10. *Gravis* is the Gramin Vikas Vigyan Samiti, or Village, Self-Help Organization founded by the late Lakshmi Tyagi and his wife, Shashi Tyagi. *Gravis* is the partner of *Wells for India* in this region.

For any reform strong leadership is needed and there are problems encountered here by the very style of leadership that is culturally acceptable. It is not only that it is male-dominated but it also prefers the guru model of leadership – and gurus are almost all men. Not only are there huge problems with succession as the guru (usually the founder) gets older, but the inability to work in a participatory and consensual manner is a hindrance to the whole organization. I have witnessed many times that everyone hangs on the words of the senior respected figure, in a way that blocks the qualities of other active, qualified members. If they speak, they may not be heard. This factor is also deeply inhibiting for women. In addition, almost to counteract some of these factors, Reform movements give birth to 'Women's Wings,' which, although they give voice to women, effectively sideline issues like water, collection of fuel, fodder and sexual violence as 'women's issues'.[11]

For example, Hugo Gorringe cites Adline, a graduate and local leader in the Madurai branch of the Women's Rights movement, who notes that

> Dalit Movements as a rule neither respect Dalit women nor use them properly.[12]

Several Dalit Women's Movements have upper-class women in leadership positions. The Dalit Liberation Movement asked for legal training for its women's wing, but its members were told by the women that it was not training that these women needed, but recognition! They were already educated and trained. This is not to undervalue for a minute, the achievements of women's group at a local level, in dealing with the money-lender, issues of violence and poverty. I have seen many women's groups in action, tackling wife-beating, alcoholism and corruption. Where there is the active support of an enlightened NGO, women can be empowered, and the very success of the action helps to build a solid identity and remove low self-esteem.

Dalit Women's Liberation Theology – Tentative Steps

It has to be admitted that Dalit Women's Liberation Theology from a strictly speaking Christian perspective is still in its infancy – that

11. Gorringe, *Untouchable Citizens*, pp. 234–35.
12. Gorringe, *Untouchable Citizens*.

is, in written form. Articles are beginning to appear in, for example, *In God's Image*, an Asian Women's Theological Journal – and elsewhere – but in general the specificity of caste has been given little attention as an area for feminist theological reflection. This calls to mind the cry of womanist theologians to Western feminists that in their focus on sexism as primary oppression, racism has become a neglected category.[13] This book has argued throughout that for Dalit women gender, class and caste oppressions are inextricably intertwined. What I attempt in this chapter is to describe the broad contours of an emerging Dalit feminist liberation theology, and then to offer some principles for how this might be developed. I focus on Christian theology, partly because this is where I am qualified, but also because there is such urgency that the Churches address this area not only in India but on an international basis. Others have already embarked upon different approaches, activist, political, neo-Buddhist and so on. Links will be made, where appropriate.

This is how Gabriele Dietrich describes the current position of Dalit theology:

> Dalit theology finds itself at the cultural crossroads between village religion and folk culture, Christianity and neo-Buddhism.[14]

If the same can also be said for Dalit *Feminist* theology, what gives the latter is specificity is the determination of Dalit woman no longer to accept the degradation forced upon her by Brahminical culture, patriarchal norms, her own men-folk and grinding poverty. Again, to cite Dietrich:

> If the victim refuses to be a victim, the power at the top of the hierarchy gets destabilised.[15]

Of course, Dalit women have always been creative in negotiating areas of freedom within the system, as I have been explaining. But a new strength is now emerging in many areas in challenging caste boundaries. And this contributes to creating self esteem and a stronger identity. As was described in the Chapter Five, the strong

---

13. For a sharp reminder of how feminist scholars can be blind to racism, see Mukti Barton's article, 'The Skin of Miriam became as white as Snow: the Challenge of the Darker Sister' in *Feminist Theology* 27(May 2001), pp. 61–80.

14. Gabriele Dietrich, 'Subversion, Transgression, Transcendence' in Gabriele Dietrich, *A New Thing on Earth* (New Delhi: ISPCK 2001) p. 242.

15. Dietrich, 'Subversion, Transgression, Transcendence', p. 239.

spirituality of Dalit women has meant that they have been able to create and sustain a vitality through their songs, stories, and in some cases by subverting patriarchy through ironically re-shaping traditional myths and narratives.[16] Some of these stories become a means of rearranging the world, in relating how women can outwit powerful men and the patriarchal system.

But if Christian theology is to play any part in enabling the liberation of Dalit women it has to be *willing to place social transformation at the heart of its theology and embody it in life-practice*. If there is a willingness to recast traditional terms like salvation and redemption with images promoting the well-being, flourishing and dignity of Dalit women, putting the struggle for survival and sustenance of the most vulnerable categories of the community as the highest priority of Church, then there is a hope that Church can *become* authentic following of Christ for the Dalit people in general and women specifically.

For Feminist Liberation theologians this means drawing on our methodologies of resistance, subversion, empowerment and visions of flourishing and making them work for the communities and contexts of Dalit women. Feminist theologians have done important work in unmasking the misogyny surrounding menstrual blood, on myths of virginity and purity, *but have not brought these into the struggle for justice for their Dalit sisters*. Nor has the extensive work on gender identity and on hearing into speech the silenced voices been put into practice. Churches – as the previous chapter indicated – urgently need to develop a listening, not only to the voices of pain and protest, the scream of Dalit women, but to the richness of Dalit women's spirituality, a spirituality that offers,

> Community instead of individualism, simplicity instead of opulence, helpfulness instead of selfishness, creativity instead of enforced mimicry, celebration instead of mere enjoyment, openness to transcendence instead of pragmatism, wisdom instead of information and naturalness instead of artificiality.[17]

What, then, are the building blocks for such a liberation theology?

16. See Franco *et al.*, *The Silken Swing*, Chapters 4–6, pp. 97–216.
17. Dr Sanjay Paswan, Dr Pramantha Jaideva, *Encyclopedia of Dalits in India, Vol. 9, Women* (Delhi: Kalpax Publications, 2002), p. 158. Also cited in writings and speeches by the El Salvadoran Liberation theologian, Rodolfo Cardenal SJ.

1. A Call to Repentance

It goes without saying that if the Church is to have authenticity for Dalit women, then a genuine journey of repentance from its replication of discriminatory structures in its own organization must be embarked on, especially where these have further oppressed Dalit women. Can the Church also develop the humility and sense of urgency to cooperate with secular movements already working far more effectively for the empowerment of Dalit women? A great range of NGOs[18] now focus on changing women's lives through their development programmes, recognizing the unique role of women in social and cultural life. As economist Amartya Sen wrote:

> Nothing, arguably, is as important today in the political economy
> of development as an adequate recognition of political, economic
> and social participation and leadership of women.[19]

Yet it is scandalous that in an institution claiming to be a means of liberating grace to the poorest of peoples, that – with a few exceptions – women's oppression is doubled. Of course, this change of heart is not confined to the Church, but to those sections of the Indian government and fundamentalist Hinduism who refuse human rights to Dalits, as well as to those sections of the Women's Movement worldwide who have chosen to remain blind to the specificity of the oppression of Dalit women.

What should urge the Church and Christianity to become dedicated to such a project, is the realization that in so doing the Church will recover the integrity of her mission to proclaim and embody the ethics of Christ's Kingdom of peace and justice. But it is never only in connection with ending discrimination that this task is urgent: the spirit, resources and faith of the Dalit people, will be the backbone of this theology's credibility, authenticity, and the touchstone of its enrichment.

2. The Theology of Dalit Women is a Liberation Theology

A liberation theology is first and foremost a theology of identification with the poorest and most vulnerable sectors of society. Sister Shalini Mulakal calls for the embodying of feminist theology at the grassroots, in this case the colonies where Dalit

18. Non-Governmental Organizations (NGOs).
19. Amartya Sen, *Development as Freedom* (Delhi: Oxford University Press, 2003), p. 203.

women live, in village or city.[20] This is the site where Dalit Feminist Theology begins. Since its inception, Feminist Theology has proclaimed women's experience as the starting point for its theology, a starting point that speaks to the specificity of her situation.[21] Dalit women experience hunger, poverty, discrimination, violence and lack of dignity in all areas of their lives. But what I have been describing in Chapter Five, 'Spirituality,' reveals Dalit women as far from passive victims: rather, they were shown to be active agents, as creatively re-shaping their myths, songs and traditions, not merely so as to survive, but to subvert the oppression of the social system.

It is this agency of Dalit women themselves that is the heart of Dalit Feminist Liberation theology. Any reflection on praxis – the essence of Liberation Theology since its inception in Latin America[22] – needs sensitivity to the life-realities of Dalit women, and needs to search for ways for their experiences to be articulated in culturally appropriate means, so that real voices are set free so as to be agents in their own struggle.

I have suggested that Dalit women are engaged in a spirituality of resistance and subversion. What is frequently missed, is that the everyday lives of Dalit women express both resistance and creativity.[23] Their lives also offer a challenge to the prevailing possessive individualism. Webs of relationships characterize their lives and identities: the level of sacrifice they willingly undergo for the well-being of children and family as subject of theology has never been explored, and, as has been suggested earlier, offers a counter-witness to the wholesale rejection of 'sacrifice' as a feminist category in the West.

3. A Liberating Reading of the Bible

James Massey and his team at the Centre for Dalit/Subaltern Studies have embarked on the ambitious process of producing Bible

20. Sister Shalini Mulakal, 'Women's Identity: Theologising at the Grassroots,' Unpublished paper, 2003.

21. This starting point has been increasingly refined to empower marginalized voices to be heard, and to ensure that the dominant voices are not European and American.

22. See Gustavo Gutiérrez, *A Theology of Liberation* (London: SCM Press, 1974).

23. Sister Shalini, 'Hunger for Food and Thirst for Dignity: Well-being as Hermeneutical Key to a Feminist Soteriology,' pp. 10–11.

commentaries of the whole Bible from a Dalit perspective.[24] This is an explicit attempt to provide a foundation for Dalit theology and to give a new and hopeful perspective to inspire peoples' life struggles. *It is particularly important to restore the text to Dalits – especially women – who may have internalized the message that reading sacred texts is for upper-caste people only.*

To move from 'subaltern consciousness' to a sense of self-esteem and empowerment is part of the process of liberation for Dalit women. Simply to make the text accessible to women is vital. And this is beginning to happen in some Christian communities. It has now become a global process that women from vulnerable sections in society – even in the midst of conflicts – discover the biblical text as liberating. Rigoberta Menchu, Nobel prize winner and an indigenous Indian from Guatemala – who was no stranger to hunger and humiliation – in the midst of the civil war, discovered this:

> We began looking for texts that represented each one of us, and tried to relate them to our Indian culture. We took the example of Moses for the men, and we have the example of Judith, who was a very famous woman in her time and appears in the Bible. She fought very hard for her people and made many attacks against the king they then had, until she finally had his head.[25]

The same process is described in African contexts. Particularly important is where women are able to use the Bible as a critical tool to address cultural issues. For example, Musimbi Kanyoro, from Kenya, who understands clearly the need for a liberating cultural hermeneutic, uses the book of Ruth to help women of her village to face unjust practices around the area of widows:

> A new insight here is that the Book of Ruth may not be only about women's happy bonding, as is said by both feminists and womanists from the west. In fact it could be about women's lives trapped in cultures. These cultures have the potential of making women compete with one another and fight each other.[26]

---

24. James Massey himself has translated the entire Bible into Punjabi.

25. Rigoberta Menchu, 'The Bible and self-Defence – the Examples of Moses, Judith and David,' in Ursula King (ed.), *Feminist Theology and the Third World: A Reader* (London: SPCK, 1994), pp. 183–88.

26. Musimbi Kanyoro, *Introducing Feminist Cultural Hermeneutics: An African Perspective* (London: Sheffield Academic Press, 2002 and Cleveland, OH: The Pilgrim Press), p. 44.

Dalit women in their turn can own the Gospel story as book that begins and ends with a woman's pain and struggle, and tells a story of the redemption of the body. For women whose bodies have been so humiliated, one of the priorities for liberation is to recover a sense of the value of their own bodies and sexuality. But, as I have been stressing, this is a task not only for women, but for the entire Church. Devashayam, (cited earlier), calls on Christian theology to engage more with Dalit religion, where male figures are subordinate to the goddess. He reminds his readers of women's sensitivity to justice issues and how important this is for the ethics of the Kingdom:

> Women by nature could be the conscience-keepers and be sensitive to the justice concerns which place them in a privileged position as agents of the Kingdom.[27]

Even if reading the Bible as liberating word had long been a mandatory process for Liberation Theology, it acquired new impetus for women with the four-fold hermeneutic of the biblical scholar, Elisabeth Schüssler Fiorenza.[28] These four steps, a hermeneutic of suspicion, proclamation, remembrance and creative actualization are full of promise for Dalit women's liberation theology. Specifically, a hermeneutic of remembrance calls on Dalit women *to re-member*, put new flesh on their identities, so trampled on by society. It is a call not only to remember the history of being independent peoples, with a pride in tradition, religion and culture; it is also a call to remember who Dalit women are as *God's good creation*, in body and spirit, created in exactly the same way as men in the image of God. And the process is now spreading like wild-fire, as Dalit Christian women discover in the prayer of Mary's Magnificat, God's promise to lift up the despised ones of the earth. And in the story of the Syro-Phoenician woman who pleaded for the healing of her mentally-stricken little girl, (Mk 7.24–30) they discover not only God's care for the racially despised, *but a woman's own agency in the healing process.* In Mary, the mother of Jesus, that bearing a child was instrumental in the redeeming of the world.

And these are only three examples.

---

27. Devashayam, *Doing Dalit Theology*, p. 61.
28. See Elisabeth Schüssler Fiorenza, *Bread not Stone: the Challenge of Feminist Biblical Interpretation* (Edinburgh: T&T Clark, 1984).

So far I have suggested a spirituality of protest, resistance and subversion and a liberating biblical hermeneutic. I want now to propose a vision of Dalit women's Liberation Theology, namely, a *vision of flourishing and wellbeing.*

4. Dalit Feminist Liberation: Visions of Flourishing

This springs from the realities of Dalit women's lives. As has already been said, Dalit women are frequently hungry. They are overworked and humiliated in the ordinary daily round. So it is not surprising to discover the idea of *well-being as salvation*, well-being not merely in the long-term, but in the present. This has been suggested by both Sister Shalini Mulakal and Fr Felix Wilfred.[29] I now want to develop this idea, using the concept of flourishing.

I begin with women's own dreams of flourishing – and first, with the *Women's Creed,* written for the United Nations Assembly at Beijing in 1995 that focused on the Rights of Women:

> Bread. A clean sky. Active peace. A woman's voice singing somewhere, melody drifting like smoke from the cook fires. The army disbanded, the harvest abundant. The wound healed, the child wanted, the prisoner freed, the body's integrity honoured, the lover returned...The labour equal, fair and valued. Delight in the challenge for consensus to solve problems. No hand raised in any gesture but greeting. Secure interiors – of heart, home, land – so firm as to make secure borders irrelevant at last. And everywhere,[30] laughter, care, dancing, contentment. A humble, earthly paradise in the *now.*

Here is the vision, embodied – true peace with justice, food in plenty, celebration, bodily integrity – all within a situation of renewed and restored just relation. Something to be celebrated as a this-worldly reality – not endlessly deferred to eternal bliss. Nor should this be dismissed as the dream only of women who are confident of worldly prosperity, and as giving up on the whole dimension of eternity, since for many women this is a crucial issue, especially

29. Mulakal, 'Hunger for Food and Thirst for Dignity,' p. 11; Fr Felix Wilfred, 'What is Wrong with Rice Christians? Well-being as Salvation – A Subaltern Perspective', in *Third Millennium IV* (2001), pp. 6–18.

30. 'A Woman's Creed' cited in Beijing Preparatory documents, and quoted in Catherine Keller, *Apocalypse now and Then* (Boston, MA: Beacon Press, 1996), p. 268. Actually it was composed by Robin Morgan with a group of Latin American Third World women sponsored by a women's Environment and Development organization.

when they experience no flourishing in this life: I suggest that the mercy of God, Sacred Being will take care of eternity. For Dalit women and those in solidarity with them, the flourishing of all creatures in the here and now is the burning issue.

And building on what Dalit women hold sacred, this is a religious vision, for it springs from the binding, connecting, sustaining of all life through sacred power and energy for its well-being. Sacred spirit, sacred energy is the source and resource for this grounded, life-giving hope.

Let us spend a moment spelling out what is meant by flourishing.[31] It is deliberately chosen as an ecological term, where body/earth/ spirit belonging together in this life-nurturing process. Flourishing means all that is life-giving for people, earth, and earth creatures together. It calls to mind many sacred texts from all faiths – important for the pluralist, multi-faith context of India: this is from the Jewish prophet Isaiah, showing how well-being of human and no-human belong together:

> The wilderness and the dry land will be glad,
> The desert shall rejoice and blossom;
> Like the crocus it shall blossom abundantly,
> and rejoice with joy and singing...
> Then the eyes of the blind shall be opened,
> And the ears of the deaf be unstopped;
> then shall the lame leap like a deer,
> and the tongue of the speechless sing for joy,
> For water shall break forth in the wilderness,
> and streams in the desert.[32]

But the text can also be adapted for the wilderness of the urban slum, often the location of Dalit colonies:

> Let the tenement and the derelict park land be glad,
> Let the slums and ghettos rejoice and burst into comfort and beauty.
> Let them flower with well-kept gardens,
> let music and laughter be heard in the streets...
> Then there will be vision for those blinded by despair,
> and the people who long for a friendly voice will hear love songs.

31. The English word is from the Latin, florere, French flourir; the German is blühen, gedeihen, which is like the English word thrive – used in a technical sense to tell if a baby will live and grow in the quality of loving care provided (Dutch bloeien, in de bloeitjd zijn, leven).

32. Isa. 35.1; 5-6.

> Those crippled with poverty will jump up and run into plenty...
> Free at last, God's people will possess the city
> and shout out in delight at God's triumph
> and their joy will last forever![33]

Second, flourishing invokes not only ecological well-being, but situates us in time and place, with all the specificity of deep-seated cultural memories, of those historical memories which constitute the identities of Dalit women. These are memories enshrined in scars, beatings and bruises, memories of always being hungry, in unwashed garments, in humiliated speechlessness; but also in the memories of courage, of survival against the odds, and of back-breaking work to prepare for celebrations that kept community pride alive.

Just as Jewish women recall the promise of Shalom, and the vision of the feast on God's holy mountain, Muslim women – in today's context of the oppression of women in many countries – remember the kindness of Mohammed towards Islamic women, within a vision of flourishing:

> God hath promised to believers,
> Men and women, Gardens
> Under which rivers flow,
> To swell therein,
> and beautiful mansions
> In Gardens of everlasting bliss.
> But the greatest bliss
> is the Good pleasure of God.[34]

If Christians remember the promise of Jesus that 'I came so that you may have life in the full', (John 10), Dalit Christian *women* now call for the *re-membering* of this in their own lives, insisting on honesty and truth-telling in the acknowledgement of the lack of honour, the lack of integrity given to their bodies. One of the most powerful calls for honour and respect to women's bodies comes from the novel, almost a sacred text, *Beloved* by the black American novelist

33. Heather Pencavel, 'An Urban Version of Isaiah 35' in Geoffrey Duncan (ed.), *Wisdom is Calling: An Anthology of Hope: An Agenda for Change* (Norwich: Canterbury Press, 1999), pp. 20–21.

34. From Surah 9: At-Taubah: 71–72; The Holy Qur'an 461, cited in Rifat Hassan, 'Muslim Women in Post-Patriarchal Islam,' in Paula M. Cooey *et al.*, (eds), *After Patriarchy: Feminist Transformations of the World Religions* (Maryknoll, NY: Orbis Books, 1992), pp. 52–53.

Toni Morrison. This is the voice of the grandmother, Baby Suggs, who has a priestly role in the book:

> She did not tell them to clean up their lives and go and sin no more. She did not tell them that they were the blessed of the earth, its inheriting meek or its glory bound pure.
>
> She told them that the only grace they could have was the grace they could imagine. That if they could not see it, they would not have it.
>
> "Here," she said, "in this here place, we flesh; flesh that weeps, laughs; flesh that dances on bare feet in grass; Love it. Love it hard. Yonder they do not love your flesh. They despise it. They don't love your eyes; they'd just as soon pick 'em out. No more do they love the skin on your back. Yonder they flay it. And O my people they do not love your hands. Those they only use, tie, bind, chop off and leave empty. Love your hands! Love them. Raise them up and kiss them. Touch others with them...And no, they ain't in love with your mouth. Yonder, out there, they will see it broken and break it again. What you say out of it they will not heed. When you scream from it they do not hear. What you put in to nourish your body they heart had to say...[35]

It is hard to find a story of such power, where suffering bodies are so cherished, here in the brokenness and oppression of the slavery of the black community. I propose it here as a text of healing, applicable to the humiliated and violated bodies of Dalit women.

Jesus' desire that vulnerable people will experience life to the full has practical expression in the present. Sister Shalini Mulakal recalls that Jesus took the initiative to feed the hungry:

> For Jesus, food and the meal had an important place in life. That is why he takes the bread as a symbol of himself and requested his disciples to break and share the bread as a remembrance of him. Dalit women's struggle to get food and share it in their family is constitutive of salvation.[36]

She points out that in kneading, baking and sharing bread – or chapatis – they become channels of salvation for others. So, why is there no acknowledgment and celebration of the eucharistic grace that Dalit women embody every day? The meal is the meeting point of various sorts of hungering, desiring and thirsting. Eating *can* be sacred space where people can flourish – yet how is this to happen

---

35. Toni Morrison, *Beloved* (London: Picador, 1988), pp. 88–89.
36. Shalini, 'Hunger for Food,' pp. 12–13.

in a context of world hunger and famine in a growing number of countries, where women struggle to give their children only one meagre meal a day?

The tradition of the sacred meal is a strong one in all faiths, in indigenous and tribal religion cerebrations. It is a time for the memory of origins and beginnings, of pride in this identity as well as the celebration of sacred moments and beloved ancestors. But it is also the convergence of pleasure in eating, the smell and taste of food, sheer sensuousness, mingled with the intimacy of being with people who form our intimate circles – all of this is part of the experience of flourishing.

Yet Dalit people – especially Dalit women – have frequently become alienated from this heritage. Accustomed to the long struggle to find sufficient food just for survival, or to the humiliation of being thrown left-overs by high-caste landowners or employers, as is frequently related, how are they to experience the reality of flourishing? Their own agency and determination is beyond question. The spiritual contribution *for the whole Church* of the daily struggle of Dalit women to feed their families needs to be recognized and valued in parish communities and theological circles. This would be a first yet vital step in the journey to flourishing.

Third, flourishing as a root metaphor has the power to call us out of the old symbolic system, (or set of symbols), on which patriarchy depends.[37] Patriarchal power, seen as domination over women, children, the vulnerable, and indigenous peoples deprived of land, depends above all on *militarism and violence*. Thousands of raped women all over the world witness to this fact, to the way women's bodies continue to be sacrificed to the war machine – and this book has made it clear that for Dalit women it is *the caste war* that is here the relevant category.

Violence thrives on *disconnection* – of people from the earth, of humanity from all sensitivity to suffering. Militarism not only devises earth-destroying and polluting weapons but ensures that those who should be sowing and harvesting crops are fleeing for their lives. And finally, militarism thrives on a culture of secrecy and lies. Keeping wars going means money and jobs for some. Cultures

37. This is developed in a systematic way by the late Grace Jantzen, in the context of philosophy of Religion, *Becoming Divine* (London: Routledge, 1998). And in an ecological context by Chris J. Cuomo, *Feminism and Ecological Communities: An Ethic of Flourishing* (London: Routledge, 1998).

depending for livelihood in exporting arms to Third World countries, and governments who buy them – instead of feeding their people – are cultures devoted to death, not life.

Yet, all the major religions, indigenous and tribal traditions, and new forms of religion emerging from ecofeminism and from the recovery of forgotten traditions contain dimensions of *life-giving* processes – even if submerged in dominant interpretations. Grace Jantzen uses the term 'natality' ('Natalité') in contrast with 'mortality,' that is, birth-giving or creativity as opposed to the death-dealing aspects of patriarchy. Birth-giving is meant here in a wider sense than biological birth: it includes the well-being and focus on justice for mothers and all who care for children. It also stirs the imagination and energy towards the creation of a system of cultural symbols enabling the well-being and flourishing of women – and, by extension, a logic of flourishing for all.

Thus, under the traditional symbolic system in Christianity, salvation through Jesus is the preferred symbol offering us freedom from death, guilt, sin, punishment, Hell. But, in practice, because of the prevailing culture of militarism and violence, this has – as we have seen – involved the sacrificing of women's bodies, all too often justified as being linked with sin, death and mortality. Indeed, some of the fathers of the Church, offered salvation and sanctity to women if they rejected the female body and were regarded as 'honorary men'. St Augustine – North African Bishop of the fifth century – in his 'City Of God', did allow that women would go to Heaven, but that what was characteristically female, that is, having a womb, would be transformed into a higher use.[38]

We know, too, that women have inscribed or internalized in their bodies the blame, the guilt for sin. They have endured beatings from husbands and men-folk and felt they deserved it. They have internalized the command to obey, to be subservient, to keep domestic peace, and seen even their own sons adopt 'the rule of the father' in the name of religion. We have already noted this in the context of Dalit women. And in the name of a religion where becoming divine was the privilege reserved only for men. Even though in theory, all human beings are called to be just and compassionate, and in Christianity and Judaism, both men and women are created in the image of God, religion as expressed in

38. Augustine, *City of God*, Ch. 22.

society sees the male as expressing the Divine image par excellence, and the genealogy as passing between father and son. Woman is merely the vessel, the bearer of the seed for the future. Could another symbol-system based on creativity, birth-giving offer the visions – and modest utopias – of flourishing we seek?

Such a symbol-system would offer the re-valuing of the female body and female sexuality as part of a process of restoring the goodness of mutuality and intimacy to women and men. Recovering redemptive intimacy is part of flourishing. It is uncovering the authentic roots of desire. It means recognizing that there is no flourishing for anyone where the bodies of children and women are sexually violated in rape, abuse, or forced prostitution. Rediscovering the sacredness of sexuality is part of experiencing being created in the image of God, as God's good creation, called to become divine. Yearning for the realization of this is an integral part of salvation imaged as flourishing.

An important part of this is re-thinking the value of work. The least valued types of work have been heaped onto Dalit people and especially Dalit women, as I have shown. And yet this is work vital to the well-being and flourishing of the whole community. It is not enough to share the humble work of sweeping, housework and cleaning. The whole system of valuing people in a hierarchical system that despises the lower rungs must be rejected and the harsh dualism underpinning it exposed and expunged. This was what Gandhi actually hoped would happen in his ashrams.

But, the powerful creation traditions – often deeply hidden – of our own faith resources point the way. Christians, for example, re-image Jesus as the pattern which connects: he is as an embodiment of the healing pattern of just relationship. The ethical visions of all great faiths – Buddhist compassion, the genuine teaching of Mohammed, the Hindu scripture's stress on the sacredness of creation, Jewish faithfulness to Halakkah (the laws governing daily life) – all of these need to be tested for the truth of whether they offer genuine flourishing for Dalit women. If not, we must say so and reject them. We call as a resource upon the imagery of Spirit-Sophia, Spirit-Wisdom, the female Divine principle revealed in the Bible. Moving in and out of all faiths and religions, connecting and re-connecting with forgotten traditions and lost hopes, Holy Wisdom opens up the possibilities of flourishing and recovery of dignity for Dalit women and all Dalit people.

Conclusion: The Many Paths to Freedom

The Jewish/Islamic religious concept of Shalom/Salaam encapsulates much of what is meant by flourishing. This suggests the weaving together of all the strands I discussed – justice and mercy in politics, a peace celebrated deep in the heart, a peace with one's own body – though it may be ageing, and far from the fashion icons of beauty trumpeted by culture; an end to violence against all vulnerable people; a sense of joy and hope for the future redemption of culture, when as the Book of Revelation tells us,

> the leaves of the tree of life are for the healing of the nations.[39]

As the Chipko story revealed, and as Chapter Five has argued, the wisdom of Dalit women is rooted in the belief in the interconnectedness of the well-being of trees, plants, seeds and people. It is a wisdom to be respected if there is to be a liberation of culture for all peoples.

I have now opened up a predominantly Christian theological vision of flourishing as part of the Liberation struggle for Dalit women: it keeps alive the vision that empowered them at the 2004 World Social Forum – 'another world is possible'. But it cannot stand alone in pluralist India. I now ask what is the enduring contribution to the struggle of the Indian reformers themselves, especially of Gandhi and Ambedkar.

39. Revelation 22.

Chapter 8

OPPOSITION TO UNTOUCHABILITY – THE KEY INSPIRATION OF LEADERS OF REFORM MOVEMENTS

You and your husband have rightly been excommunicated. You help the lowly castes like the *mangs* and *mahars* and that, undoubtedly, is committing sin. You have dragged our family name in the mud. Therefore, I want to tell you that you must behave according to the customs of our caste, and follow the dictates of the Brahmins – (The accusation of Savitribai Phule's brother against her).[1]

The achievement of Independence would go to the credit of Mahatmaji, and its codification to one of Mahatamaji's worst critics, viz., the great architect of our great Constitution, Dr Ambedkar. Dr Ambedkar, Sir, deserves not only the gratitude of this Assembly, but of this nation– Syamandam Sayar, of Bihar.[2]

Liberation for the Dalit people will include many strands, not only because of the obduracy and long-lasting nature of caste oppression, but because of the pluriform, diverse nature and built-in structures of resistance of Asian society. The history of caste oppression has been sketched but not the history of efforts to reform it. Many contemporary efforts still draw strength and inspiration from the past, from individuals and their followers as well as from different faiths and movements. This chapter first looks at some key figures, especially those who continue to inspire women today and at some religious reform movements that arose partly in protest against caste, such as Buddhism. Second, the Chapter considers the enduring influence of the Dalit leader Dr Ambedkar, asking why he chose to leave Hinduism, and looking specifically at the enduring impact on women of his conversion to Buddhism. Third, I re-examine the

1. Cited in Susie Tharu and K. Lalita (eds), *Women Writing in India, Vol. 1*, 'Letter to Jyotiba Phule, 10th October 1856' (New Delhi: Oxford University Press, 1991), pp. 213.
2. James Massey, *Dr B.R. Ambedkar: A Study in Just Society* (New Delhi: Manohar, Centre for Dalit Studies, 2003), pp. 75–76.

tensions between Mahatma Gandhi and Dr Ambedkar, asking if the legacy of Gandhi – despite the bitter opposition between the two leaders in their lifetime, and resentment of contemporary Dalits towards Gandhi – still offers strength to the struggle of Dalit women for dignity and Human Rights. I will argue that both leaders are important, and that the Dalit struggle needs to hold on to the legacy and inspiration of both figures. Specifically, it will be important to judge if their respective positions can be reconciled.

Singling out specific figures can be invidious: but I hope these can be placed within a constellation of inspiring people, including local deities, the poets of the Bhakti (devotional) movement, like Ravidas and Mirabai, as well as the countless unsung heroes/ heroines who have sustain the courage of their communities in the struggle for survival and dignity over the centuries.

Savitribai Phule – Revered Role Model for Dalit Women

Savitribai Phule is first presented because she, (with her husband), continues to be an inspiring role model for Dalit women. Born in January 1831 in India at Naigon, she married Jyotirao Phule when she was only nine years old and he was twelve. This was a common practice at the time – and, as has been already noted, child marriage remains a grave justice issue in many parts of India. Encouraged by her husband to get an education, Savitribai began her journey towards the emancipation of the women-folk of her village in 1841.[3] She was one of the first girls to achieve Higher Education

A postage stamp issued by the Indian Government in Savitribai Phule's honour, 10 March 1998.

3. See http://www.mahatmaphule.com/savitribaiphule.html. This section is dependent on this article. The postage stamp image is from the same source.

in Modern India and the first to become a school teacher. There is no doubt that she would not have been able to achieve what she did without the active support of her husband Jyotirao (or Jyotiba, as he is usually known). This is hardly surprising: the same phenomenon is true of many European women who sought to make their way in a male-dominated world in the nineteenth century, George Eliot (Mary Ann Evans), to cite one example. Even in emancipated India today, married women (especially Brahmin women), find it almost impossible to achieve their professional ambitions without the support of their husbands.

Savitribai's husband, Jyotirao (hence Jyotiba) is regarded as one of the most important figures in social reform movements in Maharashtra and India, especially for his efforts to educate women and the lower castes. In Maharashtra these were the *Mangs* and *Mahars*. The Mahars were the largest caste in this state, and were important village servants:

> They carried messages, guided strangers and assisted the headman. They also guarded the boundaries of the villages and kept it clean. Besides, they also settled land disputes for they were living reference books of village and family history and contemporary social relations.[4]

Neither of the Phules ever referred to them as *Untouchables*. Jyotiba became Savitribai's mentor and supporter and under his influence she took on as the mission of her life the goals of women's education and liberation from the cultural patterns of male-dominated society. She worked towards tackling some major social problems including women's liberation, the remarriage of widows and the removal of untouchability. Both husband and wife were reviled by the upper-castes and even by their own families for their public opposition to Untouchability (as the harsh quotation above has shown). Savitribai's reply to her brother was so eloquent that her mother exclaimed:

> Savitri, the goddess Saraswati herself must be speaking through your mouth. I feel intensely satisfied to listen to your wisdom.[5]

Jyotiba, working for women's education had started the first girl's school and, requiring women teachers to assist him, educated and trained his wife. But they both faced fierce resistance from orthodox

4. Irawait Karve, cited in Tharu and Lalita (eds), *Women Writing in India*, p. 211.
5. Karve, cited in Tharu and Lalita (eds), *Women Writing in India*, p. 214.

elements of society and had to separate from the family of their in-laws under this pressure. After Savitribai graduated from her Training College with flying colours (along with a Muslim woman Fatima Sheikh), with her husband, she opened five schools in and around Pune in 1848, one being for girls of the Mang and Mahar caste. With Fatima Sheikh she would teach here until 1856. The degree of harassment can be judged by the fact that even the journey to school was an ordeal for Savitribai: groups of orthodox men would follow her, abusing her in obscene language and throwing rotten eggs, cow dung, tomatoes and stones at her.

> Orthodox society was not prepared for this "misadventure", as women's education was frowned upon. It was believed that if a woman starts writing she would write letters to all. People claimed that the food her husband ate would turn into worms and she would lose him by his untimely death.[6]

However, despite all these oppositions, Savitribai persevered, continued to teach the children and was ultimately honoured by the British for her educational work. (The ambiguous position of the British with regard to Untouchability should be noted, and will be returned to in connection with Ambedkar. Many reformers at this time looked to the British government in the hope that they would support reform).

Their efforts in the area of the remarriage of widows were equally revolutionary. Because of the custom of arranging marriages between young girls and old men, frequently men would die of old age or illness and their young child-brides were left widows. (Death through military engagement was also common). Often the woman was blamed for her husband's death and thought to bring bad luck. Thus, widows were not expected to use cosmetics or to look beautiful: their heads were shaved, they wore the simplest of saris and were compelled by society to lead an ascetic life. Beggary or prostitution became a common fate. Savitribai and Jyotiba, moved by the plight of such widows, castigated the barbers and organized a strike of barbers, persuading them not to shave the heads of widows. (This was the first strike of its kind). Thus Savitribai was not only involved in educational activities but also in every social struggle launched by Jyotiba. Once he stopped a pregnant woman from committing suicide, promising her to give

6. www.mahatmaphule.com/savitribaiphule.html

her child his name after it was born. Savitribai accepted the woman into her house, assured her of her help in the delivery, later adopting the child. As an adult this same child became a doctor and on the occasion of Jyotiba's death, he set light to his funeral pyre, thus completing the traditional duties of a rightful son. This incident created new awareness for Savitribai and her husband as to another aspect of the plight of widows in Hindu society. They saw how many women were driven to commit suicide by men who had exploited them for their own ends, and then deserted them. So they created a 'Delivery Home' for women on whom pregnancy had been forced. They also fought against all forms of social prejudices. Upset to see Untouchables being refused drinking water meant for the upper-caste, (which has been discussed in an earlier chapter as a continuing injustice), they opened up a reservoir of water for the Untouchables in the precincts of their own house. They were also opposed to idolatry, and championed the cause of peasants and workers, always facing social isolation and vicious attacks from people whom they questioned.

But their most enduring reform was the formation of the Movement, Satya Shodak Samaj (Society of Seekers of Truth) on 24 September 1873, with Jyotiba as first president. Every member had to take a pledge of loyalty to the British Empire.[7] The main objectives of the organization were to liberate the Shudras and to prevent their exploitation by the Brahmins. All the members of the Satya Shodhak Samaj were expected to treat all human beings as children of God and worship the Creator without the help of any mediator. Membership was open to all and the movement grew quickly: in 1876 there were 316 members. After Jyotiba's death, Savitribai took over the responsibility of Satya Shodhak, presiding over meetings and guiding its workers. At a severe outbreak of the plague Savitribai worked night and day for its victims, organizing camps for poor children. It is said that she used to feed two thousand children every day during the epidemic. By a sad irony, she herself was struck by the same disease while nursing a sick child and died on 10 March 1897.

It is because of her enduring legacy and influence that her story has been told. First, Savitribai's poems and other writings are still an inspiration to many. In fact, she was a pioneer of Marathi poetry

7. The different attitude of Dalits to the British Empire, as contrasted with those who worked for India's independence, will be discussed below.

(see the anthology, *Poisoned Bread*, mentioned elsewhere in this book),[8] her poems dealing with a range of social issues, including decrying the caste system, and poems about nature and the benefits of education. Her letters give a window into the experiences of women during social movement, a movement that had a strong impact, and attracted other reformers. Her legacy is also seen in Pune, where *The Krantijyoti Savitribai Phule Women's Studies Centre* is located in the University of Pune, a city with a long lineage of political consciousness and political activism for the human rights of women: this Women Studies Centre is still known for its commitment to excellence and innovation. Finally, Savitribai has been recognized by the State Government as a significant figure: the Maharashtra government has established an award in her name, for *Women Who Work for Social Causes.*

Periyar E.V. Ramasamy

The third figure to be mentioned, taking us almost into contemporary times, is Periyar E.V. Ramasamy, (referred to hence as simply Periyar, or 'respected elder'): he deserves mention because of his long political life of campaigning for the rights of the Dalit people and his opposition – at times, violent – to Brahmanism. Like Gandhi and Ambedkar, he has been involved in all the key historical events both before and after India's Independence. He is a precursor to the discussion as to whether justice could be achieved for Dalits while remaining within Hinduism. Hugo Gorringe considers Periyar's legacy a vital factor in improving the position of women in Tamil Nadu:

> Tamil Nadu figures prominently as a 'success story' of fertility decline, partly due to the history of Periyar's Self-Respect Movement (SRM) which insisted on the equality and autonomy of women.[9]

Born in Erode, Tamil Nadu, Periyar joined the Indian National Congress in 1919, but resigned in 1925 when he felt that the party was only serving the interests of the Brahmins. In 1924, he led a

---

8. Arjun Dangle (ed.), *Poisoned Bread: Translations from Modern Marathi Dalit Literature* (Hyderabad: Orient Longman, 1992).

9. Hugo Gorringe, *Untouchable Citizens: Dalit Movements and Democratisation in Tamil Nadu* (New Delhi: Sage Publications, 2005), p. 220.

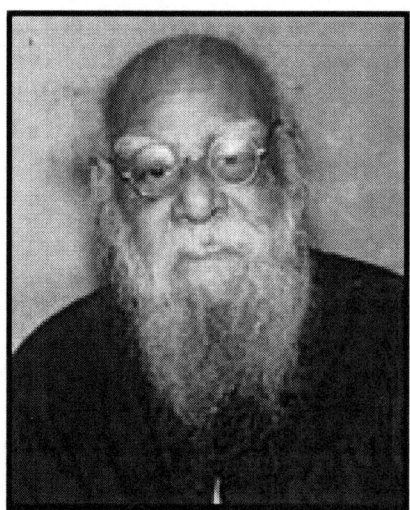

Periyar E.V. Ramasamy, 1973[10]

non-violent agitation (*satyagraha*[11]) in Kerala. From 1929 to 1932 he toured Malaysia, Europe, and Russia, which had an influence on him. In 1939, Periyar became the head of the Justice Party, and in 1944, he changed its name to *Dravidar Kazhagam*. (The Dravidians of Tamil Nadu are considered to be the original inhabitants of South India). While continuing the *Self-Respect Movement*, he advocated for an independent Dravida Nadu which he wanted to call *Dravidistan*.

Periyar propagated the principles of rationalism, self-respect, women's rights and eradication of caste. He opposed the exploitation and marginalization of the non-Brahmin indigenous Dravidian peoples of South India and the imposition of, what he considered to be *Indo-Aryan India*. His work has greatly revolutionized Tamil society. Two aspects of his work will be discussed, the *satyagraha* that took place in Vaikom, and the enduring influence for women of the movement he founded, the Self-Respect Movement.

The Satyagraha at Vaikom (1924–1925)

Vaikom is a small town in Kerala state, called Travancore at this time. Here there were strict laws of untouchability in and around

10. Photo courtesy of Wikipedia.
11. This would become an important tool for Gandhi's Reform.

the temple area. *Dalits*, also known then as Harijans, (the name given to them by Gandhi, which they reject), were not allowed into the streets around and leading to the temple, let alone inside it. Here anti-caste feelings were growing steadily and in 1924 Vaikom was chosen as a suitable place for an organized *Satyagraha*, the name given to the peaceful resistance campaign as practiced by Gandhi. Under his guidance a movement had already begun with the aim of giving all castes the right to enter the temples. Thus, agitations and demonstrations took place. On 14 April, Periyar and his wife Nagamma arrived in Vaikom and were met with arrest and imprisonment for their participation. In spite of Gandhi's objection to non-Keralites and non-Hindus taking part, Periyar and his followers continued to give support to the movement until it was withdrawn. He received the title *Vikkom Veeran*, mostly given by his Tamil followers who participated in the action.[12]

The way in which the *Vaikom Satyagraha* events have been recorded provides a clue to the image of the respective organizers. Yet various sources make no mention of Periyar: however, his vital contribution through the Self-Respect Movement cannot be denied.

Self-Respect Movement

During the early years of the Self-Respect Movement Periyar and his followers campaigned constantly to influence and pressurize the government to take measures for removing social inequality, while other nationalist forerunners focused on the struggle for political independence. The Self-Respect Movement was described from the beginning, as dedicated to the goal of giving non-Brahmins a sense of pride based in their Dravidian past. In 1952, the Periyar *Self-Respect Movement Institution* was registered with a list of radical and ambitious objectives which included:

12. A considerable section of intellectuals feel that Periyar's participation in the Indian independence movement and his contribution in the Vaikom Satyagraha have been highly exaggerated. For example, Eleanor Zelliot, a history professor and a respected authority on Gandhi and Ambedkar, in her article entitled *Gandhi and Ambedkar, A Study in Leadership*, tells the story of the 'Vaikom Satyagraha' including Gandhi's negotiations with the temple authorities in relation to the event – but Periyar is given no great role. In fact, the editor of Periyar's *Thoughts* states that Brahmins purposely suppressed news about Periyar's participation. A leading Congress magazine, *Young India*, in its extensive reports on Vaikom never mentions Periyar.

- the spread of knowledge useful for political education;
- allowing people to live a life of freedom from slavery to anything that blocked reason and self-respect; to do away with needless customs, meaningless ceremonies and blind superstitious beliefs in society;
- to put an end to the present social system in which caste, religion, community and traditional occupations based on the accident of birth, have chained the mass of the people and created 'superior' and 'inferior' classes...and to give people equal rights; to completely eradicate untouchability and to establish a united society based on brotherhood and sisterhood;
- to give equal rights to women;
- to prevent child marriages and marriages based on law favourable to one sect, to conduct and encourage love marriages, widow marriages, inter-caste and inter-religious marriages and to have the marriages registered under the Civil Law;
- to establish and maintain homes for orphans and widows, and to run educational institutions.

How successful was this ambitious programme? Certainly the propagation of the philosophy of *self-respect* became Periyar's full-time programme after 1925. The Movement began to grow rapidly and right from the beginning received the sympathy of the heads of the Justice Party. In May 1929, a conference of Self-Respect Volunteers was held at Pattukkotai and Conferences followed in succession throughout Tamil Nadu. A training school in Self-Respect was opened at Erode, Periyar's home town. The object was not just to introduce social reform but to bring about a social revolution to foster a new spirit and build a new society. It was not an easy task for Periyar to create this awakening among people who had, for generations, become used to their subordinate position – the internalization of inferiority referred to earlier. Periyar spoke to the people on innumerable platforms over the years to arouse their thinking power. His whole approach was based on the power of reason. He thought all were born with this, but few knew how to use their innate powers! Periyar's foremost appeal to people was to develop self-respect. He preached that the Brahmins have monopolized and cheated other communities for decades and deprived them of self-respect. He continually reminded them that most Brahmins claimed to belong to a 'superior' community with the reserved privilege of being in charge of temples. He felt that they were trying to reassert their control over religion by using their superior caste status to claim the exclusive privilege to touch idols or enter sacred shrines and temples. He claimed that in certain places the scheduled caste people were not allowed to use the tanks, wells and at times even the streets used by Brahmins. Periyar remained active in politics throughout his long life, in the Justice Party, and its successor, after the former was split. Here I focus on his achievements in the areas of caste and Women's Rights.

Women's Rights

Throughout his life Periyar advocated forcefully that women should be given their legitimate position in society as the equals of men and that they should be a given good education and also the right to property: he was keen that women should realize these rights and become worthy citizens of their country. So he fought against the orthodox traditions of marriage as a means of the suppression of women in Tamil Nadu and throughout the entire Indian sub-continent. As Gorringe relates, he divested women's reproductive role within marriage of its religious aura and linked it with a this-worldly dynamics.[13] Though arranged marriages were meant to enable a couple to live together for a lifetime, in fact they were manipulated to keep women in a state of slavery. Child marriage was the worst example of this. It was actually believed that it would be a sin to marry after puberty. Another practice, still prevalent today, is the dowry system where the bride's family is supposed to give the husband a huge payment for the bride. The original purpose of this had been to assist the newly wedded couple financially, but in many instances dowries were misused by bridegrooms and their families. The outcome of this often resulted in the exploitation of the bride's parents wealth, and in certain circumstances, lead to dowry deaths. (Although, as I have noted earlier, dowry abuse is more common in upper-caste families, or today in cases where upwardly mobile Dalit families are imitating practices of the upper-castes). There have been hundreds of thousands of cases where wives have been murdered, mutilated, and burned alive because the bride's father was unable to make the dowry payment to the

13. Gorringe, *Untouchable Citizens*, p. 220, citing S. Anandhi, 'Reproductive Bodies and Regulated Sexuality,' in M. John and J. Nair (eds), *A Question of Silence?* (London: Zed Books, 1998), pp. 139–66. Citation p. 153.

husband. This abuse was fiercely opposed by Periyar. He also fought for the property rights of women, the right of women to work outside the home, and also advocated that women have the right to separate or divorce their husbands in certain circumstances. At a time when birth control remained taboo in society, he campaigned for it not only for the sake of women's health and population control, but also that they should have control over their bodies and be free from domination. Now 50 years later, in a context where India's population growth gives cause for great concern, many States are encouraging this policy, advocated half a century ago by Periyar. Not only did Periyar campaign for just wages for women, but even that there should be a wage given for housework!

What was also remarkable was his criticism of double standards in the area of sexual purity, arguing that chastity should also either belong to men, or not at all for both individuals. While fighting against this, Periyar advocated getting rid of the Devadasi system of temple prostitution (discussed earlier). As a further example of liberation of women, Periyar pushed for the right of women to join the armed services and the police force. It is beyond dispute that Periyar and the Self-Respect movement achieved a better status for women in Tamil society – the evidence of this is seen by the number of young women in higher education in subjects like engineering and medicine.

His attitude to religion was governed by his ideas of reform. Periyar's philosophy did not differentiate social and political service. According to him, the first duty of a government is to run the social organization efficiently, and the philosophy of religion was to organize the social system. He pointed out that while Christian and Islamic religions were fulfilling this role, the Hindu religion remained totally unsuitable for social progress. As regards the caste system, Periyar felt that a small number of cunning people had created caste distinctions in order to dominate over society. Hence his emphasis on developing self-respect and learning to analyse propositions rationally:

> A self-respecting rationalist will readily realize that caste system has been stifling self-respect and therefore he will strive to get rid of this menace.[14]

14. Anita Diehl. *E.V. Ramasamy Naiker-Periyar* (Sweden: Scandinavian University Books, 1977), p. 19.

Like views cited earlier, Periyar believed that the caste system in south India is, due to Indo-Aryan influence, linked with the arrival of Brahmins from the north. Periyar also mentions that birds, animals, and worms, which are considered to be devoid of rationalism, do not create castes, or differences of high and low in their own species. But men and women, considered to be rational beings, are suffering from distinctions because of religion. He further explains that amongst dogs you do not have a Brahmin dog, or a Pariah (untouchable) dog. *Among donkeys and monkeys we also do not find such things. But, amongst men there is such discrimination.*

Yet Periyar was not against Hinduism as such. When accused of attacking Hinduism and the Brahmin community he explained that it was Brahminism and not Brahmins that was the problem, and the manipulation of Hinduism and not Hinduism as a faith. His emphasis was always on rational behaviour and he felt that some people used religion only as a mask to deceive innocent people: it was his life's mission to warn people against superstitions and the hypocrisy of priests. Periyar openly suggested to those who were marginalized within Hindu communities that they should consider converting to other faiths such as Islam, Christianity, or Buddhism. He found in Buddhism a basis for his philosophy though he did not accept that religion, seeing it rather as an alternative in the search for self-respect, with the object of getting liberation from the discrimination of Hinduism. Periyar commended Islam for its belief in one invisible and formless God, proclamation of equal rights for men and women; and advocating of social unity. But, as we shall see, it was to Buddhism that the great Dalit reformer Ambedkar would turn. There were many differences between Gandhi and Periyar, as we shall see. Suffice it to say that, despite many controversial aspects as to Periyar's methods, (including the fact that they were sometimes violent), the impact of Periyar's reforms especially for women is still in evidence today especially in Tamil Nadu – (though Gorringe considers that talk about women's rights remains largely rhetorical)[15] – even if he did not achieve his aim of an independent Dravidistan!

15. Gorringe, *Untouchable Citizens*, p. 221.

Buddhism and neo-Buddhism: Its Promise for Dalits

Buddhism is the next discussion area, mostly because of its key role in the life and followers of Dr Ambedkar. Arising in India and once dominant through much of the country, Buddhism had begun to decline by the twelfth century. However, its revival began in India in 1891, when the Sri Lankan Buddhist leader Anagarika Dharmapala founded the Maha Bodhi Society.[16] This attracted mainly upper-caste people. Then, in 1890, the Sakya Buddhist Society was founded by Pandit C. Ayodhya Dasa (1845–1914). It was also known as the Indian Buddhist Association.[17] The important point for this narrative – focusing on what this means for Dalits – is that Thass, a Tamil Siddha physician, was the pioneer of the Tamil Dalit Movement. He argued that Tamil Dalits were originally Buddhists and led a delegation of prominent Dalits to Henry Steel Olcott (1832–1907), the founder and first president of the Theosophical Society and first well-known European to convert to Buddhism. Thass asked for his help in the reestablishment of 'Tamil Buddhism.' He then established the *Sakya Buddhist Society* in Madras (Chennai) with branches in many places including Karnataka, as well as a weekly magazine in Chennai in 1907, which served as a newsletter linking all the new branches of the Sakya Buddhist Society. The magazine discussed traditions and practices of Tamil Buddhism, new developments in the Buddhist world, and the Indian subcontinent's history from the Buddhist point of view. Brahmananda Reddy, a Dalit leader from Andhra Pradesh, was also fascinated by Buddhism and history indicates that this fascination was mirrored by developments in many parts of India.[18] The story takes a decisive turn with the life-long struggles of Dr Ambedkar.

16. The source here is www.wikipedia.wiki.Dalit_Buddhist_movement, as well as Tharu and Lalita (eds), *Women Writing in India*, pp. 211–13.

17. The first president of the Indian Buddhist Association was the German born American Paul Carus, the author of *The Gospel of Buddha* (London: The Merchant Book Company, 1995 [1894]).

18. In the early twentieth century, the Barua Buddhists of Bengal under the leadership of Kripasaran Mahasthavir (1865–1926), founder of the Bengal Buddhist Association, Calcutta (1892) established viharas in cities such as Lucknow, Hyderabad, Shillong and Jamshedpur. In Lucknow, Bodhanand Mahastavir (1874–1952) advocated Buddhism for Dalits. Born Mukund Prakash in a Bengali Brahmin family, he was orphaned at a young age, and was then raised in Benaras by an aunt. He was initially attracted to Christianity, but became a Buddhist after a meeting with Buddhist monks from Ceylon at a

Dr Babasaheb Ambedkar

Ambedkar has been mentioned many times in this book as a Dalit hero and leader, as involved in the creation of India's first constitution, and for his lasting importance for the Dalit Movement. His views on the origins of Untouchability have also been cited. The focus here is, first, on his conversion to Buddhism, second, its lasting effects and impact, and third, on the question as to whether his bitter dispute with Gandhi is so serious that the latter and his reforms can be said to hold no promise for Dalits, and in particular, Dalit women. Ambedkar's conversion to Buddhism was a process that took over 20 years and involved his bitter disputes with Gandhi over the formation of the Indian constitution. There were many differences between the two leaders: not the least is because Gandhi brought religion into politics, refusing to separate personal from political life, and Ambedkar hoped to solve the dispute rationally. In fact, Ambedkar – here, reminiscent of Periyar – thought Gandhi a man of high principles but not rationality, and he hoped to solve all disputes within a legal framework.[19]

Ambedkar's Conversion

At the Yeola conference in 1935, Dr B.R. Ambedkar, declared that he would not die a Hindu, saying that Hinduism perpetuates caste injustices. He was approached by various leaders of different denominations and faiths. Meetings were held to discuss the question of Dalit religion and the pros and cons of conversion. On 22 May 1936, an 'All Religious Conference' was held at Lucknow,

Theosophical Conference in Benares. He later lived in Lucknow where he came in contact with Barua Buddhists, many of whom were employed as cooks by the British. In 1914, Prakash was ordained Bodhanand Mahastavir in Calcutta in the presence of Kripasaran Mahasthvir. He began preaching Buddhism in Lucknow. He founded the *Bharatiye Buddh Samiti* in 1916, and set up a vihara in 1928. In his book *Original Inhabitants and Aryans*, Mahastavir stated that the shudras were the original inhabitants of India, who were enslaved by the Aryans. Source is Maren Bellwinkel-Schempp, 'Roots of Ambedkar Buddhism in Kanpur,' in Surendra Jondhale and Johannes Beltz, *Reconstructing the World: B.R. Ambedkar and Buddhism in India* (New Delhi: Oxford University Press, 2004), pp. 221–44. See http://www.maren-bellwinkel.de/artikel/ambedkarbuddhism.pdf

19. A.K. Vakil, *Gandhi-Ambedkar Dispute: An Analytical Study* (New Delhi: Ashish Publishing House, 1991), p. 7.

attended by prominent Dalit leaders, though Ambedkar could not attend it. At the conference, Muslim, Christian, Sikh, and Buddhist representatives presented the tenets of their respective religions in an effort to win over Dalits – and we have already seen the complexities of conversion to Christianity and how this proceeded over the centuries.

The Buddhist monk, Lokanatha, visited Ambedkar's home on 10 June 1936 and tried to persuade him to embrace Buddhism. Later in an interview to the Press, Lokanatha said that Ambedkar was impressed with Buddhism and that his own ambition was to convert all Dalits to Buddhism. In 1937 Lokanatha published a pamphlet *Buddhism Will Make You Free*, dedicated to the Depressed Classes of India from his press in Ceylon. In the early 1940s, Ambedkar visited Acharya Ishvardatt Medharthi's Buddhpuri school in Kanpur. (Medharthi had earlier been initiated into Buddhism by Lokanatha, and by the mid-1940s, he had close contacts with Ambedkar). Meetings between Ambedkar and prominent Buddhists continued.

After publishing a series of books and articles arguing that Buddhism was the only way for the Untouchables to gain equality, Ambedkar ended the process of 21 years and publicly converted on 14 October 1956, at Nagpur. He took the Three Refuges and the Five Precepts from a Buddhist monk, Bhadant U Chandramani, in the traditional manner[20] and then in his turn administered them to the 380,000 of his followers who were present. Here is how he described his decision:

> I started the movement of renouncing the Hindu Religion in 1935 at Nasik, and since then have been continuing the struggle. A mammoth meeting was held at Yevala, in 1935 in which through a resolution a decision was taken to the effect that we should renounce the Hindu religion. In that meeting I had said that though born a Hindu because I could not help it, I would not die a Hindu. This conversion has given me enormous satisfaction and pleasure unimaginable. I feel as if I had been liberated from Hell.[21]

20. The 3 Refuges (or Jewels) of Buddhism are: Buddha, Dharma (teaching) and Sangha (Community); The 5 Precepts are: I will be mindful of all life; I will respect the property of others; I will be conscious and loving in my relationships; I will honour honesty and truth; I will exercise proper care over my body and mind.
21. Cited in James Massey, Dr B.R. Ambedkar, *A Study in Just Society* (New Delhi: Manohar Publishers/Centre for Dalit Studies, 2003), p. 39.

Ambedkar, already a sick man, would die less than two months later, just after finishing his definitive work on Buddhism. Many Dalits employ the term 'Ambedkar(ite) Buddhism' to designate the Buddhist movement, which started with Ambedkar's conversion and many converted people called themselves as 'Nava-Buddha' that is, New Buddhists.[22]

Twenty-two Vows of Ambedkar

After receiving his ordination, Ambedkar gave *dhamma diksha* (initiation teachings) to his followers. The ceremony included 22 vows given to all new converts after the 3 Jewels and 5 Precepts. On the 16 October 1956, Ambedkar performed another mass religious conversion ceremony at Chanda and prescribed 22 vows to his followers.[23] Nowadays many Ambedkarite Organizations are working for these 22 vows, believing that these vows only are responsible for the existence and rapid growth of contemporary Buddhism in India.

But the words of Ambedkar, as he closed his speech at Nagpur, urging his followers to 'educate, organise, agitate' were to have lasting significance: many believe the focus should be on 'organise' and that it has been the failure to do this that has paralysed many Dalit Movements in inaction.

Dalit Buddhism Movement After Ambedkar's Death – A Lasting Influence?

The Buddhist movement received a severe setback at Dr Ambedkar's death so tragically soon after his conversion. Unfortunately, his action did not receive immediate mass support from the Untouchable population that Ambedkar had hoped for. Division and lack of direction among the leaders of the Ambedkarite movement have been an additional impediment. According to the 2001 census, there are currently 7.95m Buddhists in India, at least 5.83m of whom are Buddhists in Maharashtra. This makes Buddhism the fifth-largest religion in India but less than 1 percent of the overall population of India. Not all Buddhists are Ambedkarites (or followers of Ambedkar). But many are, within and outside India.

22. This section follows www.en.wikipedia.dalit_movment.org
23. See Appendix C for the text.

A prominent group in Maharashtra, called Trailokya Bau Mahasangha Sahayak Gana, (TBMSG), a Buddhist Sangha,[24] discovered by Valerie Mason-John, impressed her by the number of women who witnessed to how their lives had changed by converting to Buddhism and working for TBMSG:

> My conversion has given me a direction for my life. It's come at a time when all my sons have turned 18, so I can fully commit to the emancipation of the Dalits in India. My husband talks about organisation, education and agitation. I hope to do this for the freedom of the Dalit people throughout India.[25]

There are many such moving stories of conversion. TBMSG was founded by Bhante Urgyen Sangharakshita, founder of the Western Buddhist Order in England. TBMSG works spiritually through practising loving-kindness and learning Buddhist ways of relating. Then its devotees – and especially women –become empowered to engage in social work in their communities. Ambedkar's vision is believed to be the necessity of conversion not only for Dalits but for all Indians. Only thus can caste-ism be eradicated. The legacy of Ambedkar's conversion to Buddhism for Dalit women can also be judged by the fact that Meera Ambedkar, his daughter-in-law was chosen as President of the Indian Buddhist Association in 1977: she is completely devoted to carrying on his work. In the 29 years of her Presidency[26] she has given more than 14 retreats a year, experiences that have begun to transform the lives of women.[27]

Gandhi's Legacy

If Dr Ambedkar is the chosen hero of Dalits, why dwell longer on Gandhi? My principal reason is because I observe contemporary Gandhian movements on the ground are of key significance in transforming the lives of Dalit women and poor rural communities. Second, because I have seen Gandhi unjustly criticized and dismissed by Dalit Movements, without any consideration of what he actually achieved.

24. *Sangha* is the term for a community of practising Buddhists.
25. Valerie Mason-John, *Broken Voices: Untouchable Women Speak Out* (New Delhi: India Research Press, 2008), p.194.
26. Of course, this will be a few years more on the publication of this book.
27. Valerie Mason-John, *Broken Voices*, pp. 244–48.

The origins of the dispute are well-known and it is not my intention to retrace well-known territory. It is absolutely true that Ambedkar's key political role in the creation of the constitution and his efforts to eradicate Untouchability have been eclipsed over the years by the international fame of the Mahatma. Only recently have attempts to redress the balance been made. Yet, to this day anniversaries of Ambedkar's birth and death – crucial for Ambedkarites – are not celebrated nationally in India in the same way as those of Gandhi. It is also true that Gandhi made what appear to be dreadful (when taken out of context) remarks about Untouchables some of which have already been cited.[28]

The heart of the bitterness of the Dalit people centred on Gandhi's refusal to allow a separate vote for Dalits in the new Constitution (although he himself had also envisaged this in the beginning). He saw it as essential to maintain Hindu unity as adequate balance to the Muslim vote. From the distance of 60 years it is possible to respect his deep concern for holding the country together, and his sense of broken-heartedness at the tragedy of Partition, a wound felt up to this day. He felt this as a personal failure. It was his decision to fast unto death that caused Ambedkar to give up his own wish for a separate vote, and set in motion a lasting Dalit enmity towards Gandhi.

It is true that their positions on caste were poles apart. Gandhi found caste-ism distressing, even abhorrent, an 'excrescence' of Hinduism and wanted its reform. He undertook a thorough reform programme in his ashrams, where all were to share the humblest of tasks – such as cleaning latrines. His ethics were focused on the poorest and most vulnerable sectors of society – that included Dalits (or Harijans, as he called them) but were not exclusive to Dalits. Women were a particular concern. Their well-being was crucial to his ideas on education, on the future of children and on the viability of the Village Republic. Gandhi – as contrasted with Nehru and his five-year plans – saw the village as the heart of India's development. He knew that the villages needed a degree of self-sufficiency and self-reliance, but to many, this appeared to be against progress.[29]

28. For example, his remarks idealizing the Bhangi woman.
29. See V.B. Eswaran, 'Gandhiji, Government and the Rural Poor,' in Anton Copley and George Paxton (eds), *Gandhi and the Contemporary World* (Chennai: Indo-British Historical Society, 1997), pp. 129–38.

But all his efforts were embedded within the context of Hinduism, which, after years of study, he considered to be a more superior religion than others he had studied, like Islam and Christianity. By contrast, Ambedkar – who scoffed at Gandhi's proposals – saw caste-ism as fundamental to Hinduism and, along with prominent Dalit leaders, wanted it completely destroyed. Removing Untouchability would only strengthen Hinduism, he thought.[30] Some believe that the tensions between the two were caused by clashing personalities and by the urgency of the programme for the formation of the constitution. As A.K. Vakil summarized the situation:

> If Gandhi could have found some more time from his busy political schedule, he would have been successful in abolishing Untouchability. Ambedkar's mission of awakening the Untouchables while removing Untouchability was unparalleled. If he could have followed the non-violence way of *satyagraha*, though it could have demanded of him more sacrifice and forbearance, it could have been more fruitful in the long run.[31]

Conclusion

As we have seen, Ambedkar's legacy is vital for the Dalit Movement. But so, I would argue, is Gandhi's. *Satyagraha* continues to be an active, non-violent movement of protest against injustice across many areas of oppression. Gandhian NGO's – such as *Gravis*, mentioned several times in this book – continue to be active not only for the flourishing of the rural poor, but for justice across caste barriers. Even the government of India, despite the temptations of money pouring in from the World Bank for large development schemes, is aware of the severe problems arising from its neglect of the villages. It is now actively trying to fund watershed regeneration schemes that will bring about water security for remote and poor villages.

The relevance for this book of both these legacies is that both leaders harnessed religious resources for the ending of caste discrimination. Ambedkar, after a 30 year struggle within Hinduism left a legacy via Buddhist practice; Gandhi, even if his sincere

30. A.K. Vakil, *Gandhi and Ambedkar Dispute*, p. 51.
31. Vakil, *Gandhi and Ambedkar Dispute*, p. 78.

efforts to reform Untouchability are now seen as insufficiently radical, yet through his ethics of non-violence, he left a way of reaching out to the very poorest and most vulnerable of people, within a vision of reconciliation for the country itself. And this is still seen as inspirational across the world.

Chapter 9

The Way Forward – Seeking a Transformed Future

The term Dalit consciousness stands for change and revolution. By using the term Dalit women we are trying to say that if women from Dalit castes and Dalit consciousness create a space for themselves for fearless expression, ie. if they become subjects or agents or self, they will provide a new leadership to Indian society in general, and to feminists and Dalit Movements in particular – Vidyut Bhagwat.[1]

It is time to take stock. The picture this book has been painting does not admit an easy solution, rather an ambiguous situation. There is definitely no ambiguity as to the severity of oppression, brutality and humiliation suffered by Dalit people and women in particular. This was sketched in the first three chapters. The ambiguity arises in asking whether religion can provide any solution, when it is so clearly part of the problem in the first place. Chapters 4–7 attempted to highlight some of the strengths of religion for Dalit women as well as some of its negative features, particularly the way caste-ism is backed by religiously-sanctioned societal stratification.

The first point is to acknowledge the definite progress that has been made. Many Dalit women are educated and hold professional jobs in many key areas. Some are involved in political parties. But with the notable exception of a few key activists like Ruth Manorama, there is still a dearth of Dalit women leaders – and very few Dalit women theologians. And the area of greatest stress and suffering are India's many villages, especially remote areas, as well as in the city slums. Here, Dalit women are still vulnerable to the atrocities and humiliations that this book has been describing. It should be noted that, whereas the rest of the world sees India as a success story in economic terms, *yet a third of the world's billion poor live in*

1. Italics are in the original. Vidyut Bhagwat, 'Dalit Women: Issues and Perspectives: Some Critical Reflections' in P.G. Jogdand (ed.), *Dalit Women – Issues and Perspectives* (Pune: Gyan Publishing House, 1995), p. 2.

India, and the majority of these are Dalits. So, while the overall picture acknowledges progress, much more needs to be achieved, especially in the way that caste and gender oppression coincide in the lives of Dalit women. New areas of suffering have been generated for Dalit communities and especially women by the policies of global capitalism, as I have argued. The question I raise is, how far can religion be part of the solution, if at all?

An International Human Rights Issue

Great political figures – like both Gandhi and Ambedkar in their different ways – the leaders of the social movements of the nineteenth century, (like Periyar's Self-Respect Movement) have all struggled to remove the burden of Untouchability. There are now many movements engaged in the struggle. Where some have been ineffective in the past, the difference now is that Dalit issues and caste oppression are recognised as international Human Rights issues, no longer merely internal issues for India's government and institutions. This is not only because of the gravity of caste oppression in India, but because the same issues are present in Nepal, Pakistan and Sri Lanka: indeed they followed Indians to Britain. This means that no one deeply concerned with justice can ignore the situation. But, despite this, not only is injustice against Dalit communities still unrecognized in many circles, but a specific focus on the situation of Dalit *women* on national and international levels has gained very little attention.

The Needs of Dalit Women as an Issue for International Human Rights

This book has already stressed the need for access to education for Dalit women and girls, especially basic literacy, and to basis sources of sustenance like water and fodder. This has to be recognized as a basic International Human Rights issue – as for example, was flagged up in the Social Forum at Mumbai 2004. Educational programmes, formal and informal, need to be focused on what will actually empower Dalit women as well as making education a safe experience for Dalit children.

In our own (i.e. *Wells for India*) projects in Rajasthan the single most effective action for liberation is the creation of Self-Help

Groups (SHGs) for women. Seen as vital for income-generation, they also are a means of building confidence, self-esteem and leadership among rural women. I have also observed them functioning to overcome caste barriers, since women from all castes are gathered together on the same carpet, discussing issues and problems that face them all. This is specifically encouraged by Gandhians.[2]

But even before education, the right to life is the first basic human right. It has been observed that among Scheduled Castes that there is a higher incidence of female infanticide than among the rest of the population and this must be related to both caste and gender oppression.

It is also important, as I have been arguing, to applaud and encourage the numerous movements of Dalit women mobilized in their own struggle for human rights. Basically, the struggle for liberation will be achieved by Dalit women themselves: the role of outsiders is to be in solidarity, and to facilitate the voices, stories and struggles of Dalit women in being heard at an international level.

As Vimal Thorat has written in an encouraging tone:

> Nevertheless, the Dalit women's articulations are growing. After the formation of the NFDW in 1995, (National Federation of Dalit Women) there have been two conferences in Dhule and in Mumbai, 1997 (that was opposed by the Shiv Sena), three in Delhi and two in Chennai. Our ranks are swelling. There is great enthusiasm for the movement.

> We believe that only after these distinct articulations are made and space created for our voices and issues that a broader alliance will get forged again. We have been kept out, left behind, denied by our own movement (the Dalit Movement) and also by the Women's Movement.[3]

What is referred to here on a national basis also occurs in every Dalit colony. Countless Dalit women's groups are mushrooming. But not all of them are equally effective. First, the attempts of Dalit women to be active in the political arena are fraught with danger: as Vimal Thorat noted:

2. Of course, these are situated within a wider programme of programmes for water provision, health and child education.

3. Vimal Thorat, 'Dalit Women Today' *Communalism Combat* (May 2001), Cover story.

In Sonipat, Haryana the elected *sarpanch* (District Council leader) who is a Dalit woman has been forcibly denied entry by caste bullies. She will pollute the *panchayat* office (=District Council Office) if she enters, they say! What is the Dalit political leadership, the rest of the political leadership and the Women's Movement, doing about this? No one has even raised the issue let alone supporting it …

Two years back, in a similar incident in Madhya Pradesh, an elected Dalit woman *sarpanch* was stripped and paraded around the village for daring to hoist the Indian flag. Civil liberties organisations took up the issue but where were the RPI, the BSP, the Women's Movement then?[4]

Condemnation of such atrocities must be taken up and condemned at international level, if it proves that injustice cannot be attained locally. Second, what may also happen is that rural less-educated women may be active in picketing, write the authors of The *Encyclopaedia of Dalits in India*, whereas,

Dalits in higher echelons favoured political participation but non-violent methods.[5]

They note the tendency to leave politics for other women to continue the pursuit of achievement of higher status.[6] This points to the many kinds of solidarity needed for effective social change, not the least being the awareness of the Women's Movement that the issues being campaigned for may *not* be the crucial ones for Dalit women. What needs highlighting is the fact that Dalit women's progress to full participation in Indian society is now blocked by new violence caused by a mixture of Hindu right wing nationalism, giving patriarchal norms a pernicious virulence, and the damaging effects on Dalit women of globalization policies. These two factors alone make the issue of survival, dignity, and basic Human Rights for Dalit women an international one that cannot be assumed to be the task of Indian groups alone.

The kind of solidarity needed is to support, especially financially, Centres for Dalit Human Rights, where they exist in India and elsewhere, in their campaigns for achieving justice in the law courts

4. Thorat, 'Dalit Women Today.'

5. Dr Sanjay Paswan and Dr Pramantha Jaideva, *Encyclopedia of Dalits in India, Vol 9, Women* (Delhi: Kalpax Publications, 2002), p. 143.

6. Paswan and Jaideva, *Encyclopedia of Dalits in India*, p. 149.

for atrocities against Dalit women and their communities.[7] Second, supporting Dalit-led NGOs is vital, especially where their policies are to empower women. Third, if national campaigns cooperate with indigenous Indian movements, this can work for consciousness-raising and for social change. Thus in the UK Dalit Solidarity Network (DSN)[8] works with the International Dalit Solidarity Network (IDSN) to ensure just employment principles in Banks and other Corporations (outsourced to India) through the acceptance of the Ambedkar Principles, and other awareness raising activities, such as Early Day motions in the House of Commons, London, and raising issues in the European Parliament. The most recent campaign is to work with the Indian NGO, Safai Karmachari Andolan (SKA) to end the practice of manual scavenging (described earlier in connection with the Bhangi people)[9] by the Commonwealth Games in 2010 (See Appendix B). The aim is to persuade the Indian Government to release the money already earmarked to end scavenging by this time, noting that the practice, still deeply entrenched, has been illegal since 1993.

Issues for the Church and Pastoral Theology

The ambiguity surrounding the importance of religion for Dalit women as regards Christianity, centred on the experience of Christianity as reinforcing subordination and increasing their burdens. The contemporary context of Christians in India is now far from easy. Violence against Christians and the threat of anti-conversion legal measures has created a climate of danger and fear in certain places.[10] In 2007, for example, 50,000 Christians were driven out of their homes in Orissa.

Far from criticizing all that has occurred in the past, I want to harness all that is good about the Christian Church to work for the liberation of Dalit women. Far from criticizing the missionaries, it

7. The Centre for Dalit Human Rights in Jaipur, Rajasthan, is extremely active in monitoring and pursuing justice in hundreds of these cases. They are funded by Dan-Aid, Denmark.

8. This was founded by Revd David Haslam in 1997.

9. It should be noted that the Bhangis are only one out of many Dalit communities engaged in this practice.

10. See Joshua Newton, 'Government Aims to Stop Low-caste Hindus from Embracing Islam, Christianity', http://www.hrwf.net

is salutary to note what they did achieve for the improvement of the lives of Dalit communities. Yet Dalit theologians like James Massey think it is time to shake off a certain dependency on the missionaries. It is beyond question that the efforts of so many religious congregations – including the Delhi Brotherhood, the Jesuits, and many congregations of Roman Catholic religious sisters, who struggle tirelessly for justice for Dalits and specifically for Dalit women, are making vital contributions. Yet it may now be timely to recognize that Christian Church can be most effective when cooperating with secular movements as described above.

Yet Church structures cannot be left off the hook: what is still needed is a commitment from the churches' hierarchies (the Catholic Bishops hierarchy, the Church of North and South India – and so on) to end caste discrimination in the experience of lived Christian life. *And to mirror this commitment in their own structures by the appointment of Dalit leaders in authoritative positions.* Each of us, in whatever country we are, needs to join in solidarity to urge the leaders of our own Churches to bring pressure on the Indian churches to take effective action on these issues. It is important to recognize certain achievements through government initiatives, the work of NGOs and solidarity of some Church organizations such as VODI (*Voices of Dalit International*), who are attempting to work in this cooperative way. A recent conference (July 2009) organized by Voice of Dalit International in London, addressed caste discrimination in the UK, where around 50 delegates from different Faith and Community groups, Human Rights organizations, Churches, Charities, Aid Agencies and the Media assembled at the venue of the Catholic Association for Racial Justice, achieving a joint statement condemning caste discrimination with many conclusions and commitments, especially to act on the following declaration:

1. Caste Discrimination exists in the UK and needs to be outlawed.
2. Caste Discrimination is practiced by Asian communities in the UK, irrespective of religious beliefs.
3. Caste Discrimination is against the cherished values of the UK – democracy, human rights, equality, social cohesion etc.

Church groups and agencies should also support the efforts of activists who challenge the rules against inter-dining and intermarriage. (We have already noted that the closure of the marriage circle is closely intertwined with the origins of caste hierarchy).

It requires great courage in dealing with Bishops' hierarchies in different countries: the badge of authentication of this challenge is the question as to whether the leaders of Christian Churches are prepared to commit themselves to Jesus' identification with the poorest and most vulnerable in society. *It is the burning and inescapable question of Christian integrity.*

These words are but meaningless symbols without action. And that's the test – dedicated action on many fronts. If the Church wants to be seen as living witness to Christian integrity, she must address not only the discrimination issue within her own congregations, not only the violence and oppressed situation of Dalit women in society but she must be proactive on the educational front. This means positively promoting the education of Dalit girls, from childhood through to the highest levels. It means, subsequently, enabling their employment in Church committees, commissions, in schools, hospitals and in seminaries – recognizing the church's enormous investment in education and in social and pastoral institutions. It also means tackling key issues in the curriculum; in the recent past, enormous attention has been devoted to Karl Marx and then to Gandhi – but how much to Ambedkar? Interfaith study now includes Hinduism and Islam – but not the religion of the Dalit people? If Dalit Theology is the indigenous Liberation Theology of India, then *Dalit women's Liberation Theology is its hidden face.* How can seminary formation remain ignorant of its message?

It could also be said that the church's pastoral role has in the past been its pride and strength. Only faith communities across the spectrum have consistently practised care, diakonia, (διάκονια) to the poor and outcaste of the earth as part of their mission.[11] Today, pastoral care for Dalit communities needs to focus not only on practical and ethical issues, but on the deeper issues of shame and wounded psyche, that have been an undercurrent throughout this work.[12] The long-endured trauma of Dalit people, and especially Dalit women can only be healed by transforming strategies at many levels – by respect, by positive affirmation, by worship that

11. The Sikh community in Delhi, in its large temple in the centre of New Delhi, feeds about 5,000 people a day.

12. See John Webster, *Religion and Dalit Liberation: An Examination of Perspectives* (New Delhi: Manohar, 2002), Chapter 7, pp. 119–47.

addresses the realities of their lives, by enabling the dignity and flourishing that is their human right. Christianity once knew how to do this in its origins, when poor and landless people found themselves affirmed by belonging to a community empowered to proclaim the coming Kingdom of justice and peace (Lk. 4.18–30).

Yet it still seems that there is an elephant in the room. This is the fact that Caste-ism can still be undergirded by a strictly conservative reading of Hinduism. Whatever is achieved by international solidarity and human rights, by education, whatever degree of humility Christian Churches attain in repenting of their complicity in discrimination, the full eradication of the caste system can only be achieved by Hindu religious leaders themselves. Perhaps by slowly letting go of its rigid marriage systems, its prohibition of inter-dining, and by re-examining its notions of purity and pollution, Hinduism will discover a new and greater truth that will promote the wellbeing of all its adherents and show to the world that caste-ism, like slavery can be dismantled for the mutual benefit of all.

Global Society is now in a changing economic climate: though Globalization seems overwhelming in its grasp,[13] and India is becoming a key economic player, Liberation Theology, beginning in Latin America, *is now here to stay* in its diverse acculturated forms, in different continents. It is has been recognized that Liberation Theology came late to recognize the oppression of women and that of the earth. It has come at an even later hour to recognize the oppression of Dalit women. But as yet, a passionate commitment to eradicate this has yet to be seen. But I want to give the last word to the courage, protest and dreams of Dalit women themselves, from whatever faith and life-situation they come:

> Woe to you the politicians,
> You sided with the upper-castes;
> Your power will be curtailed;
>
> Woe to you the police,
> You harassed us unnecessarily;
> You will be buried alive.
>
> Woe to you the Dalit leaders,
> You sold us for your survival,
> Your security will be shattered.....

13. At the time of writing, it is uncertain how the current economic crisis will end.

Blessed the Dalit women,
For you will mother the
martyrs of Dalitsthan.

Blessed are you the activists,
You shall be rewarded
for your commitment.
Blessed are the Dalits,

For you will create a
Dalitsthan,
From your burnt-out ashes.[14]

If justice and flourishing for Dalit women and their communities can be achieved without further martyrs, without ashes and without further violence, this would be a great sign of hope for India's future.

14. Paswan and Jaideva, *Encyclopedia of Dalits in India*, pp. 161–62.

AMBEDKAR PRINCIPLES

International Dalit Solidarity Network

WORKING GLOBALLY AGAINST DISCRIMINATION BASED ON WORK AND DESCENT

THE AMBEDKAR PRINCIPLES*

EMPLOYMENT AND ADDITIONAL PRINCIPLES ON ECONOMIC AND SOCIAL EXCLUSION FORMULATED TO ASSIST ALL FOREIGN INVESTORS IN SOUTH ASIA TO ADDRESS CASTE DISCRIMINATION

1. Caste discrimination remains a serious problem in the countries of South Asia. The Principles outlined below are an attempt to address this. They are intended to acknowledge the degree of historic injustice against Dalits and to compensate for this through **affirmative action**, in line with international Human Rights standards, although not to the detriment of other excluded groups. They will enable foreign investors or companies trading in the region to contribute to eliminating caste discrimination in the labour market. Much has been learned from the use of similar principles aiming to create equality in employment, such as the Wood-Sheppard Principles in the UK and the MacBride Principles in Northern Ireland – relating to racial and religious discrimination respectively - and from principles developed in relation to investment in countries with serious and structural human rights violations, such as the EU Code of Conduct and the Sullivan Principles drawn up in the 1970s to address apartheid in South Africa.

2. The main **Employment Principles** are firmly rooted in and seek to build upon the labour rights that are already supported by the international community - governments, trade unions and employers' associations alike - in the form of the conventions of the International Labour Organisation (ILO). They can be seen as the practical application of a number of these rights for a large section of the South Asian population that has been subjugated for centuries. These people are severely discriminated against even today on the basis of being born into a particular 'caste' or social group.

3. At present the obligations of states with regard to implementing labour rights are increasingly being complemented by instruments that call upon the corporate sector to be responsible and accountable for its impact on the wider society, including those whom it employs or whose employment it influences through the sub-contracting chain. One of these instruments is the UN Global Compact, of which Principle 6 requires supporting companies to seek 'the elimination of discrimination in respect of employment and occupation'. Another is the Global Sullivan Principles, which state that companies will 'work with governments and communities in which we do business to improve the quality of life in those communities, their educational, cultural, economic and social well being and seek to provide training and opportunities for workers from disadvantaged backgrounds'. There are similar commitments in the OECD Guidance for Companies and the (draft) United Nations Norms on the Responsibilities of Transnational Corporations and other Business Enterprises with Regard to Human Rights. The **Additional Principles** on exclusion have also been evolved from these international standards.

4. Companies supporting the Principles are asked to give them general endorsement, to work progressively towards their implementation and to make an **annual report** on their progress as part of their diversity or corporate social responsibility reporting, and also to consider engaging in some form of external audit. The Principles are built upon the urgent need in any society for positive or affirmative action for severely and structurally disadvantaged groups.

5. In the Principles the term 'Dalits' is used, as that is the term chosen by many of the former 'untouchables', or 'Scheduled Castes' as the Indian Government refers to them. In this context 'Dalits' also includes indigenous people(s) (in India referred to as 'Scheduled Tribes'). 'Caste discrimination' is referred to by the **United Nations** as 'discrimination by work and descent', and was the subject in August 2002 of **General Recommendation 29** by the UN Committee for the Elimination of Racial Discrimination. The countries of 'South Asia' to which we refer are primarily India, Nepal, Pakistan, Bangladesh and Sri Lanka.

Employment Principles

Those who endorse the Employment Principles will be building on existing national anti-discrimination laws and policies, acting in the spirit of internationally recognized human and employment rights and putting into practice the general commitments found in international standards, as referred to above. They will:

1. Include in any statement of employment policy a reference to the unacceptability of caste discrimination and a commitment to seeking to eliminate it.

2. Develop and implement a plan of affirmative action, including training on caste discrimination for all employees and making specific reference to Dalit women, particularly where Dalits are under-represented as employees in relation to the local population.

3. Ensure the company and its suppliers comply with all national legislation, particularly in relation to bonded labour, manual scavenging and child labour, pay specific attention to the role that caste relations might play in legitimizing or covering up such forms of labour, and contribute actively to the implementation of existing anti-caste laws such as the Civil Rights Act and the Prevention of Atrocities Act.

4. Use fair recruitment, selection and career development processes, with clear objective criteria, and ensure that these processes are open to scrutiny from Dalits themselves as well as other civil society groups.

5. Take full responsibility for their workforce, both direct and sub-contracted, including the supply chain, in seeking to detect and remedy any caste discrimination in employment conditions, wages, benefits or job security.

6. Evolve comprehensive training opportunities for employees and potential recruits from Dalit communities (integrated with other staff where possible but separate where not), and including language support for English-deficient candidates, with the aim of enabling Dalit workers to fulfil their potential, and will wherever possible set targets for numbers of Dalit employees.

7. Designate a manager at a sufficiently senior level to carry out the policy who will aim, in the context of meeting business needs, to maximize the benefits of a diverse workforce and ensure that the policy, its monitoring and the related practices are carried through.

8. Develop effective monitoring and verification mechanisms of progress at the level of the individual company, and also co-operate in monitoring at the levels of sector and the state, involving Dalit representatives including women in these mechanisms.

9. Publish annually a report on progress in implementing these Principles – preferably in relation to an appropriate section of the Annual Report.

10. Appoint a specific board member with responsibility for oversight of this whole policy area.

Appendix B

DALIT SOLIDARITY NETWORK UK: FOUL PLAY

More than 270m people worldwide continue to experience discrimination based on their caste and practices linked to untouchability.

Communities severely affected are the Dalits (former untouchables) of South Asia, an estimated 3m Burakumin in Japan and caste people in West Africa.

This discrimination leads to poverty, segregation, exclusion and violence.

The UK Dalit Solidarity Network (DSN) is part of an international network campaigning for recognition of caste discrimination and action for its eradication. DSN lobbies, campaigns and educates about caste discrimination and how people can take action to end one of the greatest human rights abuses in the world today.

One third of the world's poor people are Dalit and a major threat to achieving the Millennium Development Goals is the continuation of caste discrimination.

Manual Scavenging

The majority of Dalits in South Asia live in chronic poverty and are deprived or excluded from adequate housing, health care, education, employment, sanitation, transport and from entering public spaces or places of worship.

Dalit communities experience daily insecurity, uncertainty and violence with usually no recourse to justice.

It is estimated that around 1.3m Dalits in India, mostly women, make their living through manual scavenging — a term used to describe the job of removing human excrement from dry toilets and sewers using basic tools such as thin boards, buckets and baskets, lined with sacking, carried on the head. Manual scavengers earn around 60p per month. Though this vile and inhumane practice was abolished by law in India in 1993 the practice is deeply entrenched in South Asian societies.

The British created official posts for manual scavengers. All institutions — army, railway, courts, industries and major towns were equipped with dry toilets instead of water-borne sewerage. This is not to say the British invented manual scavenging, rather they intervened to institutionalize it (Cited in *India Stinking*, Gita Ramaswamy, Navayana 2005).

Numerous pieces of legislation exist to protect and promote the rights of Dalits and workers. However these Acts are largely ignored, even by local authorities who employ thousands of Dalits as manual scavengers.

Manual scavenging is one of the most extreme forms of caste discrimination and its complicity in its continued practice is an international human rights scandal.

NO CASTE DISCRIMINATION AT THE COMMONWEALTH GAMES

Dalits face violence and intimidation when protesting or speaking out against the lack of policy implementation and the violation of their rights. Despite this threat an organization has been set up by manual scavengers in India called Safai Karmachari Andolan ëthe Liberation Movement of those employed as scavengers. They have launched an international campaign to demand an end to this practice by the Commonwealth Games, in Delhi, October 2010.

The Commonwealth Games should not be held in a country in which illegal manual scavenging continues.

DSN is launching a UK campaign Foul Play at it's AGM on 15th July 2008 in the International Year of Sanitation in solidarity with and support of the Indian campaign.

Foul Play is calling on:

- The Indian Government and state authorities to fulfil their own target to eliminate manual scavenging by 2010 and provide alternative livelihood options.
- The UK government and all involved in the Commonwealth Games to express their concern on this issue and to not go ahead with the games unless serious and concrete measures have been made to eradicate manual scavenging in Delhi and across India

- International institutions, governments, NGOs and trade unions to acknowledge manual scavenging and where feasible to support efforts to eradicate its practice, support rehabilitation, alternative livelihood and training programmes and install appropriate affordable and hygienic sanitation systems that do not rely on manual scavengers.
- UK companies working in India to ensure that this practice is not happening in any of their, or their suppliers, workplaces and to provide schemes for rehabilitation, employment or training for people currently employed as manual scavengers.

Internationalizing the issue has become inevitable in the context of an unresponsive caste ridden society and a half-hearted state that fails to implement its own Act prohibiting the practice. Although several prominent citizens and leaders have expressed dismay and disgust at the continuing practice of manual scavenging nothing significant has been done to eliminate it (Wilson Bezwada, Safai Karmachari Andolan).

To find out more about Foul Play and how you can play a part in ending this human rights scandal please join us at Parliament on July 15th or see DSN's website for regular updates.

www.dsnuk.org
Director: Meena Varma
Thomas Clarkson House,
The Stableyard,
Broomgrove Rd,
London SW9 9TL
Tel: +44 (0)20 7501 8323
Fax: +44 (0) 7738 4110
E-mail: meena.v@dsnuk.org
Registered charity number 1107022

Appendix C

THE TWENTY-TWO VOWS OF AMBEDKAR

1. I shall have no faith in Brahma, Vishnu and Maheshwara nor shall I worship them.
2. I shall have no faith in Rama and Krishna who are believed to be incarnation of God nor shall I worship them.
3. I shall have no faith in Gauri, Ganapati and other gods and goddesses of Hindus nor shall I worship them.
4. I do not believe in the incarnation of God.
5. I do not and shall not believe that Lord Buddha was the incarnation of Vishnu. I believe this to be sheer madness and false propaganda.
6. I shall not perform *Shraddha* nor shall I give *pind-dan*.
7. I shall not act in a manner violating the principles and teachings of the Buddha.
8. I shall not allow any ceremonies to be performed by Brahmins.
9. I shall believe in the equality of man.
10. I shall endeavor to establish equality.
11. I shall follow the noble eightfold path of the Buddha.
12. I shall follow the ten *mitaparas* prescribed by the Buddha.
13. I shall have compassion and loving kindness for all living beings and protect them.
14. I shall not steal.
15. I shall not tell lies.
16. I shall not commit carnal sins.
17. I shall not take intoxicants like liquor, drugs etc.
18. I shall endeavor to follow the noble eightfold path and practice compassion and loving kindness in everyday life.
19. I renounce Hinduism, which is harmful for humanity and impedes the advancement and development of humanity because it is based on inequality, and adopt Buddhism as my religion.

20. I firmly believe the Dhamma of the Buddha is the only true religion.
21. I believe that I am having a re-birth.
22. I solemnly declare and affirm that I shall hereafter lead my life according to the principles and teachings of the Buddha and his Dhamma.

BIBLIOGRAPHY

Ambedkar, B.R., *The Untouchables: Who Were They? And Why They Became Untouchables* (New Delhi: Amrit Books, 1948).
— 'Castes in India', in *Writings and Speeches, Vol. 1* (Bombay: Government of Maharashtra, 1989), p. 11.
Bama, *Karukka* (trans. Laxmi Homstrom; Chennai: Macmillan, 2000).
Barton, Mukti, 'The Skin of Miriam Became as White as Snow: The Challenge of the Darker Sister', *Feminist Theology* 27 (May 2001), pp. 61–80.
Bagwe, Anjali, *Of Woman Caste: The Experience of Gender in Rural India* (Calcutta: Stree, 1995).
Bellwinkel-Schempp, Maren, 'Roots of Ambedkar Buddhism in Kanpur' in Surendra Jondhale and Johannes, Beltz, *Reconstructing the World: B.R. Ambedkar and Buddhism in India* (New Delhi: Oxford University Press, 2004).
Bhave, Sumitra, *Pan on Fire: 8 Dalit Women Tell their Stories* (New Delhi: Indian Social Institute, 1988).
Carus, Paul, *The Gospel of Buddha* (London: The Merchant Book Company, 1995 [1894]).
Charsley, S.R. and Karanti, G.K. (eds), *Challenging Untouchability* (New Delhi: Sage Publications, 1998).
Chauduri, Maitrayee (ed.), *Feminism in India* (London: Zed Books 2004).
Christ, Carol, *The Rebirth of the Goddess* (New York: Addison-Wesley Publishing Co., 1997).
Clarke, Sathianathan, *Dalits and Christianity: Subaltern Religion and Liberation Theology in India* (Delhi: Oxford University Press, 1998).
Cooey, Paula M. *et al.*, (eds), *After Patriarchy: Feminist Transformations of the World Religions* (Maryknoll, NY: Orbis Books, 1992), pp. 52–53.
Copley, Antony and George Paxton (eds), *Gandhi and the Contemporary World* (Chennai: Indo-British Historical Society, 1997).
Cuomo, Chris J., *Feminism and Ecological Communities: An Ethic of Flourishing* (London: Routledge, 1998).
Dalrymple, W., *The Age of Kali* (New York: HarperCollins, 1998).
Daly, Mary, *Gyn/Ecology: The Metaethics of Radical Feminism* (Boston, MA: Beacon Press, 1978).
Dangle, Arjun (ed.), *Poisoned Bread: Translations from Modern Marathi Dalit Literature* (Hyderabad: Orient Longman, 1992).
Deliège, Robert, *The Untouchables of India* (trans. Nora Scott; Oxford: Berg, 1999), originally *Les Untouchables en Inde: Des Castes d'Exclus* (Paris: Editions Imago, 1995).

Devasahayam, V., *Doing Dalit Theology in Biblical Key* (Gurukul: ISPCK, 1997).

Dietrich, Gabriele, 'The Relationship Between Women's Movement and Dalit Movements: Case Study and Conceptual Analysis', in Gabriele Dietrich, *A New Thing on Earth: Hopes and Fears Facing Feminist Theology* (Delhi: ISPK for TTS, Madurai 2001), pp. 203-27.

— 'Subversion, Transgression, Transcendence: "Asian Spirituality" in the Light of Dalit and Adivasi Struggles' in Dietrich, *A New Thing on Earth*, pp. 238-50.

— 'Dalit Feminism and the Environment', *In God's Image*, 19.3 (September 2000), pp. 21-26.

Dube, Siddarth, *In the Land of Poverty: Memoirs of An Indian Family, 1947-1997* (New York: St Martin's Press, 1988).

Dumont, L., *Homo hierarchicus: Essai sur Le Système des castes* (Paris: Gallimard, 1966).

Fatima, Burnad, Speech on Dalit Women, Committee for the Elimination of Racial Discrimination, Geneva, 8-9 August 2002.

Fiorenza, Elisabeth Schüssler, *Bread not Stone: The Challenge of Feminist Biblical Interpretation* (Edinburgh: T&T Clark, 1984).

Fisher, R.J., *If the Rain Doesn't Come: An Anthropological Study of Drought and Human Ecology in Western Rajasthan* (Delhi: Manohar, 1997).

Fortune, Marie, *Sexual Violence: The Unmentionable Sin* (New York: Pilgrim Press, 1983).

Franco, Fernando, Jyotsna Macwan, Suguna Ramanathan (eds), *The Silken Swing: The Cultural Universe of Dalit Women* (Calcutta: Stree, 2000).

Freeman, James, *Untouchable: An Indian Life History* (Stanford, CA: Stanford University Press, 1979).

Gandhi, M.K., *Christian Missions: Their Place in India* (Ahmedabad: Navajivan Press, 1941).

Ghosh, G.K., and Shukla Ghosh, *Dalit Women* (New Delhi: A.P.H. Publishing Co., 1997).

Gnanadason, Aruna, 'They Heal their Bodies...They Heal the Earth,' *In God's Image* 19.2 (Sept. 2000), p. 47.

Good, A., *The Female Bridegroom: A Comparative Study of Life-Crisis Rituals in South India and Sri Lanka* (Oxford: Clarendon Press, 1990), pp. 14-15.

Goody, Jack and Tambiah, S.J, *Bridewealth and Dowry* (Cambridge: Cambridge University Press, 1973).

Gorringe, Hugo, *Untouchable Citizens: Dalit Movements and Democratisation in Tamil Nadu* (New Delhi: Sage Publications India, 2005).

Grey, M., *Redeeming the Dream: Christianity, Feminism and Redemption* (Gujurat: Sahitya Prakash, 2000).

— *Sacred Longings: Ecofeminist Theology and Globalisation* (London: SCM Press, 2003).

— *The Unheard Scream: The Struggles of Dalit Women in India* (New Delhi: Centre for Dalit/Subaltern Studies, 2004).

Grodzins Gold, Anne and Bhoju Ram Gujar, *In the Time of Trees and Sorrows: Nature, Power and Memory in Rajasthan* (New Delhi, Oxford University Press, 2002).

Guha, Ramamchandran, *India after Gandhi: The History of the World's Largest Democracy* (London: Macmillan, 2007).

Gupta, Dipankar, *Interrogating Caste: Understanding Hierarchy and Difference in Indian Society* (New Delhi: Penguin India, 2000).

Gutiérrez, Gustavo, *A Theology of Liberation* (London: SCM Press, 1974).

Hardgrave, Robert, *The Nadars of Tamil Nadu: The Political Culture of a Community in Change* (Berkeley, CA: University of California Press, 1969).

Harding, Luke, 'Sex Hell of Dalit Women Exposed', *The Guardian*, New Delhi, 9 May 2001.

Haskins, Susan, *Mary Magdalen* (London: HarperCollins, 1993).

Haslam, David, *Caste-out: The Liberation Struggle of the Dalits in India* (London: CTBI, 1999).

Ilaiah, Kancha, *Why I am not a Hindu: A Sudra Critique of Hindutva, Philosophy, Culture and Political Economy* (Calcutta: Samya, 2002 [1996], pp. 91–100.

Jaiswal, Sunira, *Caste: Origin, Function and Dimensions of Change* (New Delhi: Manohar, 1998).

Jantzen, Grace, *Becoming Divine* (London: Routledge, 1998).

Jassal, Smita Tewari, *Daughters of the Earth: Women and Land in UP* (New Delhi: Centre for Women's Development Studies, 2001).

Jayakumar, Samuel, *Dalit Consciousness and Christian Conversion* (Delhi: ISPCK, 1999).

Jeffrey, Patricia and Roger Jeffrey, *Don't Marry Me to a Ploughman: Women's Everyday Lives in Rural N. India* (Boulder, CO: Westview Press, 1991).

Jogdand, P.G. (ed.), *Dalit Women: Issues and Perspectives* (New Delhi: Gyan Publishing House, 2005).

John, M., and J. Nair (eds), *A Question of Silence?* (London: Zed Books, 1998).

John, T.K. (ed.), *Broken Among the Victims: Dalit Presence at the World Social Forum 2004* (New Delhi: Centre for Dalit/Subaltern Studies, 2004).

Joint Women's Programme, 'The Devadasi System in N. Karnataka', BANHI (1981–82).

Juergensmeyer, Mark, *Religion as Social Vision: The Movement Against Untouchability in 20th Century Punjab* (Berkeley, CA: University of California Press, 1982).

Kanyoro, Musimbi, *Introducing Feminist Cultural Hermeneutics: An African Perspective* (London: Sheffield Academic Press, Cleveland, OH: The Pilgrim Press, 2002).

King, Ursula (ed.), *Feminist Theology and the Third World: A Reader* (London: SPCK, 1994).

Kishwar, Madhu, Ruth Vanita (eds), *In Search of Answers: Indian Women's Voices from Manushi* (London: Zed Books, 1984).

Klass, Morton, *The Emergence of the South Asian Social System* (Philadelphia, PA: Institute for the Study of Human Issues, 1980).

Lerner, Gerda, *The Creation of Patriarchy* (Oxford: Oxford University Press, 1986).

Llangovan, R., 'A Dalit damned for defying her Village', http://hinduonnet.com/theHindu/2002/08/04

Lobo, Lancy, 'Visions, Illusions and Dilemmas of Dalit Christians in India,' in Ghanshysam Shah (ed.), *Dalit Identity and Politics: Cultural Subordination and the Dalit Challenge*, Vol. 2 (New Delhi: Sage Publications, 2001), pp. 242–57.

Lourdeswamy, Fr. S., *Empowerment of Dalit Christians: Equal Rights to all Dalits* (New Delhi: Centre for Dalit/Subaltern Studies, 2005).

Manorama, Ruth, *Dalit Women: Downtrodden of the Downtrodden: India Together*, 24 February 2006. See www.rightlivelihood.org

Mason-John, Valerie, *Broken Voices: Untouchable Women Speak Out* (New Delhi: India Research Press, 2008).

Massey, James, *Introducing Dalit Theology* (New Delhi: Centre for Dalit Studies, 2001).

— *Down-Trodden: The Struggle of India's Dalits for Identity, Solidarity and Liberation* (Geneva: World Council of Churches Publications, 1997).

— *Dr. B.R. Ambedkar: A Study in Just Society* (New Delhi: Manohar, 2003).

— *The Dalit Presence at the World Social Forum 2004*, in T.K. John (ed.), *Broken Among the Victims* (New Delhi: Centre for Dalit/Subaltern Studies, 2004), pp. 101–15.

Mathai, M.P., *Mahatma Gandhi's World-view* (New Delhi: Gandhi Peace Foundation, 2000).

Mehta, Rama, *Inside the Haveli* (London/Delhi: Penguin, 1994).

Menon, Nivedita (ed.), *Gender and Politics in India* (New Delhi: Oxford University Press, 1999).

Mukerji, Debashis, 'Brothel Buster', *The Week*, 25 January 1998.

Mulakal, Shalini, Sister 'Hunger for Food and Thirst for Dignity: Well-being as Hermeneutical Key to a Feminist Soteriology'. Unpublished paper.

— 'Women's Identity and Theologising at the Grassroots'. Unpublished paper.

— 'WSF 2004: A Feminist Perspective', in T.K. John (ed.), *Broken Among the Victims* (New Delhi: Centre for Dalit/Subaltern Studies, 2004), pp. 116–28.

Muthumary, Dr. J., *Dalit Women in India* , www.ambedkar.org

Oommen, George and John C.B. Webster, *Local Dalit Christian History* (New Delhi, ISPCK, 2002).

Paswan, Dr Sanjay and Dr Pramantha Jaideva, *Encyclopedia of Dalits in India*, Vol 9, *Women* (Delhi: Kalpax Publications, 2002).

Pathak, Bindeshwar, *Road to Freedom: A Sociological Study of the Abolition of Scavenging in India* (New Delhi: Motilal Banarsidass Publishing, 1991).

Pickett, J. Wasdom, *Christ's Way to India's Heart* (Lucknow: Lucknow Publishing House, 1938).

Phillips, Godfrey E., *The Outcastes' Hope or Work Among the Depressed Classes in India* (London: Baptist Missionary Society, 1915).

Plaskow, Judith, *Standing Again at Sinai: A Jewish Feminist Theology* (San Francisco, CA: Harper and Row, 1990).

Power, Carla, 'Becoming a Servant of God'! Devadasis are Dalit Women Sold into Sexual Slavery', *Newsweek*, 25 June 2000.

Raheja, Gloria Goodwin and Anne Grodzins Gold, *Listen to the Heron's Words* (Berkeley, CA: University of California Press, 1994).

Ramachandran, V., 'Needed: A Life of Dignity', *The Hindustan Times*, October 1999.

Ramaswamy, Gita, *India Stinking: Manual Scavengers in Andra Pradesh and Their Work* (Pondicherry: Navayana Publishing, 2005).

Rege, Sharmila, 'Dalit Women Talk Differently: A Critique of "Difference" and towards a Dalit Standpoint Position', in Maitrayee Chaudhuri (ed.), *Feminism in India* (London: Zed Books, 2004), pp. 211–25.

Riddle, Joanna and Rama Joshi, *Daughters of Independence: Gender, Caste and Class in India* (London: Zed Books, 1986).

Ruether, Rosemary Radford, *Gaia and God* (New York: HarperCollins 1992).

– *Sexism and God-Talk* (London: SCM Press, 1983).

Seenarine, Moses, *Dalit Women: Victims or Beneficiaries of Affirmative Action Policies in India – A Case Study*, Brown Bag Lecture, S. Asian Institute, Columbia University, 10 April 1996, pp. 1–12.

Sen, Amartya, *Development as Freedom* (Delhi: Oxford University Press, 2003).

Shah, Ghanshysam (ed.), *Dalit Identity and Politics: Cultural Subordination and the Dalit Challenge, Vol. 2* (New Delhi: Sage Publications, 2001).

Singh, S.K., *Dalit Women – Socio-economic Status and Issues* (Lucknow: New Royal Book Co., 2000).

Singh, Renuka, *Women Reborn. An Exploration of the Spirituality of Urban Women* (New Delhi: Penguin India, 1997).

Singaram, Charles, *The Question of Method in Dalit Theology: In Search of a Systematic Approach to the Practice of an Indian Liberation Theology*, Unpublished PhD Thesis, University of Birmingham, December 2004.

Sriniwas, Vika A.K. *Gandhi Ambedkar Dispute: An Analytical Study* (New Delhi: Ashish Publishing House, 1991).

Tamil Nadu Women's Forum, *Unheard Voices - Dalit Women* (Chennai: Tamil Nadu Women's Forum, 2007).

Tharu, Susie and K. Lalita, *Women Writing in India, Vol 1* (New Delhi: Oxford University Press, 1991).

Thorat, Dr Vimal, 'Dalit Women Today' *Communalism Combat*, May 2001, Cover story.

Tilak, Rajni, 'Dalit Women's Empowerment', Interview, November 2008. www.iheu.org/trackback/3327

The Hague Declaration on the Rights of Dalit Women (The Hague: November 2006).

Vakil, A.K. *Gandhi-Ambedkar Dispute* (New Delhi: Ashish Publishing House, 1991).

Webster, John C.B., *From Role to Identity: Dalit Christian Women in Transition* (Delhi: ISPCK CTE 13, 1995).

– *The Dalit Christians: A History* (New Delhi: ISPCK, 1992).

– *Religion and Dalit Liberation: An Examination of Perspectives* (New Delhi: Manohar, 2002).

Wilfred, Felix, 'What is wrong with Rice Christians? Well-being as Salvation – a Subaltern Perspective', Third *Millennium IV* (2001), pp. 6–18.

Williams, Dolores, *Sisters in the Wilderness: The Challenge of Womanist God-talk* (Maryknoll, NY: Orbis Books, 1993).

Zelliot, Eleanor, 'Dr Ambedkar and the Mahar Movement' (Doctoral Dissertation, University of Pennsylvania, 1969).

Document Sources:

Dalits and Development Aid (London: VODI, 2003).

Dalit Women in Rajasthan: *Status of Economic, Social and Cultural Rights*, A Study by the Programme on Women's Economic, Social and Cultural Rights, (PWESCR) together with the Centre for Dalit Rights, Jaipur (New Delhi: PWESCR, 2007).

The Hague Declaration on the Rights of Dalit Women, The Hague, November 2006.

Website Sources:

www.mahatmaphule.com/savitribaiphule.html
www.wikipedia.wiki.Dalit_Buddhist_movement
www.en.wikipedia.dalit_movement.org
http://hinduonnet.com/theHindu/2002/08/04: R.Llangovan, 'A Dalit damned for defying her Village.'

INDEX OF SUBJECTS

INDEX OF AUTHORS